QUILTING
FOR BEGINNERS

*The ultimate guide to learn
quilting easily step by step with nice and practical
Tips and Tricks.*

Angela Stuart

TABLE OF CONTENTS

Introduction

Q uilting is an art started a long time ago with evidence dating as far back as 3400 B.C in Egypt during the reign of Pharaoh. The word quilt is a Latin one calcita and it means a stuffed bag or sack. There is also a connection of the word to English and French dialects, with the former borrowing the name from the latter's cuilte. However, to this day, the origin of the term has not been pinned to a particular group of people. It seems like diverse cultures the world over adopted the art of making clothing and other household items through techniques such as sewing, appliqué and piercing.

Slightly over 90 years ago, archaeological findings in Mongolia were found to be dating as far back as between 100 BC and 200AD. Together with the findings were several pieces of literature relating to quilting. There were people known as crusaders who introduced quilting to Europe from the Middle East. This episode happened around the 11th Century. In those days, there were quilts known as gambesons that were the favorites of privileged personalities such as knights. The knights used them as part of their armor since the quilts were strong enough to protect them during the war. Beds were also made in those days using quilts with an earlier version of a quilt bed found in Sicily. This quilted bed dates back to the 14th Century. Did the quilt beds look anything close to the modern beds? The quilted bed was made of linen and stuffed with wool.

Quilting Objects

Quilting until the 12th century was a rarity in Europe. It was from this time that medieval objects like quilted beds started to emerge. The diversity of the quilts was seen in quilted doublet, aketon and so on. Since the 14th Century, this art became more popular and its use was spread to France, Germany, England and Italy.

It was not until the colonial period 1760 to 1800 that the quilt made its way to America's heartland. The fabric in use was blue and comprised of creatively done motifs and patterns, notably Bill Volckening among others that were primarily woven by women. Women did the weaving, spinning and designing the cloths. Being as it was, women of class could be spotted cladding elegant quilt attire. Such quilts were embroidered in fine needlework, notably the broderie perse and the medallion quilts were made for the high and mighty in the society. In those days, it was typical for quilters to use old blankets for batting such that a factor extended the lifespan and use of some older quilts.

Another feature of the 'American quilt revolution' was the use of paper to make quilts. You may be wondering how this used to work and indeed it served the purpose. Once a piece of fabric was cut, the paper was added as insulation during batting. Interestingly, due to scarcity of paper, women in particular used to reserve letters, newspaper cuttings and so on!

African-American quilt was distinct in a way that was used as a symbol of seeking liberty from slavery and a sure way of doing it was to write inspiring messages on the quilts and pass them to others . Notable individuals who made contributions of quilts include Amish Harriet Powers, herself a slave woman.

The Hawaiian quilting made a mark in quilting through their unique, voluptuous, curvaceous and classy quilts replete with appliqué patterns that took much of the quilt surface. This Hawaiian revolution dates back to the 1820s and 1870s. This art was acquired from missionaries in New England and was mostly a women trade.

CHAPTER 1:

Quilting Basics

Quilting is a fun and exciting way to bring out your creative side. It can bring personal fulfillment to people of all ages and skill levels.

Making a quilt is a hands-on experience. It can be a time-consuming process, but it is something that will give your fulfillment. The best thing to do is to take your time to learn the process. Even experts do not rush making their quilts. Try to enjoy the process and understand what you need to do in every step.

Do you think you are ready to make your own quilt?

The only way you can truly learn how to quilt is by making one. No matter how many tips you read, you will not fully understand them if you do not actually apply what you are reading. It is time to get your hands dirty. Gather your supplies and start quilting!

Elements of a Quilt

There are five elements of a quilt.

1. Quilt Top

The quilt top is comprised of the blocks that you have sewn together to create the design of your quilt. Besides the actual quilting of your quilt, this will be the most time-consuming portion of your project.

2. Batting

There are several different types of batting, which are made of different materials, such as polyester, cotton, and wool. They have different "lofts"—or thicknesses. Some are better for hand quilting, and others hold up better under the sewing machine.

3. Backing

The backing is just what it sounds like— the back of your quilt. The selection of the fabric is essential since this is the part that the recipient will cuddle under.

4. Quilting

The quilting is what holds your three layers together. It can be as intricate or as basic as you prefer.

5. Binding

The binding is what finishes your quilt. It seals the edges of the three layers of your quilt, preventing fraying and gives your quilt a clean edge all the way around.

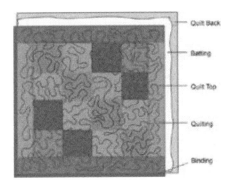

Choosing A Pattern

Beginner to Advanced: What to focus on?

Choosing a pattern will depend on what you are looking to create. Is your best friend having a baby? Is your nephew getting married? Have you been cold sitting on the couch watching TV? The style that you choose and the fabrics that will comprise your quilt will be based on the intended result.

For your first quilt or even your second, choose a pattern that is not complicated. Although we will discuss how to make triangles, avoid patterns that include them for your first couple of quilts.

Choose a pattern that has fewer pieced components. You'll have more success with the overall outcome of the quilt. A basic block quilt is the perfect place to start as a beginner.

Move slowly. Having a solid foundation of piecing will make your attempts at more complicated blocks more successful. Remember, it's not a race to the finish, but rather it's a study in detail and accuracy.

Quilt Size Chart

♥Quilt Size Chart♥

Size	width x length
Baby	36 in x 48 in
Lap	56 in x 70 in
Twin	68 in x 89 in
Full	84 in x 89 in
Queen	90 in x 84 in
King	106 in x 94 in

Basic Steps of Quilting

Here are the things that you should do. These are the considerably basic steps of quilting which could help you get started.

1. Decide on a pattern

Once you are an expert quilter, you will no longer need a pattern to come up with beautiful designs, but since you are just starting, you might want to consider using an easy pattern that can guide you with your creation. For those who are just starting, it is easier to choose a blanket made of quilted rows.

2.   Wash and press the fabric.

As mentioned earlier, you need to make sure that your fabric is perfect for your quilt even before you start sewing. You can do this by washing and pressing the fabric first.

Pre-washing will allow you to determine if your fabric will bleed or shrink. Generally speaking, the higher-quality fabric will not, but it is best to check, nonetheless. Pressing the fabric will allow for easier cutting. You do not need to press the wadding. Only the two outer layers need to be ironed.

3. Measure accordingly

Measure the size of the individual pieces that you need to complete the pattern. Do not forget to add an allowance for the seam: usually, a 1/4-inch is necessary. This means that you need to add 1/4 inch on each side of the square. For example, if the requirement is five inches per side, you need to create pieces that measure 5 1/2 inch by 5 1/2 inch. This step will be easier if you have a ruler and a washable fabric pen to mark the measurements before cutting.

4. Start cutting

Make sure you measure everything twice before cutting to avoid mistakes. If you have a rotary blade and a cutting mat, lay the fabric on top of one another on the mat and cut accordingly with the guidance of a ruler. If you are using scissors, cut the fabric one by one, and make sure that you follow the markings you made to keep the edges straight.

5. Sew the squares together

You can practice arranging the fabric and designs before you sew the cut pieces of the square together. Lay your quilt so that you can see the pattern that you are trying to create.

Pin the individual squares together so that it will be easier for you to sew. Whether you are using your hand or the machine, the point is just to sew the squares together until you come up with long, thin strips. Work your way across the quilt until you come up with one row. You can then proceed to complete the following row afterward. Make sure that you are sewing the rows together at precisely 1/4 inch. You should have several rows of squares after this step.

6. Sew the rows together

Now that you have several rows of squares, you have to sew the rows together. The process is still the same, but instead of just square pieces, you are now going to sew together the rows of square pieces that you made earlier. Work your way downward. Make sure that you are still keeping the 1/4-inch allowance for the seam. Just keep on adding rows until you complete the quilt. If you find that the square pieces do not exactly line up, it is okay. It will give your quilt a personalized touch.

You now have the front layer of your quilt.

7. Baste the quilt

Pin your quilt in place before sewing. You can use pins or a basting gun for this step. Keep the quilt you just created in front, the wadding in the middle and backing pattern at the back. Make sure that the pins are secure and try to remove any wrinkles on the quilt to make the sewing process much more comfortable.

8. Sew the layers together

Before sewing the quilt together, be sure that everything is in the right place. The more seams you sew through the quilt, the better your quilt will be because it will be hard to move. More seams will also prevent bunching up inside the quilt. You also have the option to sew the seams diagonally or to sew freehand to add a personalized touch to what you are doing. However, if you are not yet completely confident about your sewing skills, it is best to apply the pattern first.

9. Sew the binding

The binding is like the border of the fabric. Aside from adding to the aesthetic quality of your quilt, it will protect the seams and add a more finished look. It should be around 2 1/2 inches wide, and it should go around the perimeter of your quilt. For something square, cut four strips of equal length.

Before you sew the binding, pin them in place first so that it will not move around as you sew. Use as many pins as you need to secure the binding in place. Start with sewing the front of the binding. If you are using a printed binding, make sure that you are showing the printed side.

The tricky party of sewing the binding is sewing the back part because there is a chance that the stitches will show at the front. In order to prevent this, you can use an invisible thread, or you can opt to hand stitch so that the stitches will look neat. Try to avoid going through all three layers of the quilt.

As you finish the basting, make sure that you have even seams. You should also check if the corners are squared off.

10. Wash your quilt

Your quilt is now finished!

Before using it, wash it first so that it will have a soft and vintage feel. It will also allow you to see if you will encounter any problems before using the quilt. Now you can admire your work and be proud of yourself for finishing your very own handmade quilt.

CHAPTER 2:

Quilting Tools

Before you can start quilting, you should make sure that you have everything you need to do the job correctly. You can buy many of the tools required to create a functional quilt from a general store, but you can also try specialty stores and ask the sales assistant if you are getting the right tools or equipment for your quilting project.

Every creator needs tools for making masterpieces. Quilting is no different. People who want to create beautiful quilts that can be passed down through generations need to have the following tools in their arsenal:

Sewing Machine

The first thing a quilter needs is a sewing machine, though this wouldn't be necessary if she is already adept at hand sewing. However, those who are not too confident about their hand sewing skills would have to invest in a sewing machine. The sewing machine that you invest in doesn't have to be highly expensive as long as the quality is good and it does the job well.

Also, most expensive sewing machines are equipped with unusual stitch patterns. This feature wouldn't be necessary since quilting often requires a simple straight stitch. These high-end machines might also be a little complicated for beginners. Based on user evaluations and tips from other experts, beginners have to look for the following qualities on the sewing machine that they plan to buy:

• Affordable – as earlier mentioned, the price of sewing machines often varies according to the features that come with it. While choosing from various brands of primary sewing machines, it is usually best to stick with the brands that are slightly more expensive than the rest. That's because these machines are often more durable than their counterparts and also come with better service warranties.

• Easy to use – the most significant consideration for beginners should be the ease by which the sewing machine can be threaded. This is because incorrect threading may lead to problems with the thread while the machine is running. These problems include bunching, breaking, and looping. Most machines come with step-by-step instructions on how to properly wind the bobbin and run the thread through the needle. Be sure to follow the steps accurately so as not to encounter any issues in the future.

• Reliable – simply put, the sewing machine has to deliver as promised. The machine that you choose for quilting should be able to produce the same quality of the stitches through several layers of fabric.

Scissors

These are necessary for every type of sewing job. However, one thing that you have to remember about sewing scissors is that scissors used for cutting fabric should never be used to cut any other non-fabric material. Doing so would dull the edges of the scissors, making them useless for cutting fabric. This is especially true if the fabric scissors are used for cutting paper. Since quilting requires cutting fabric and paper designs, it is best to have two different pairs of scissors for each purpose.

Another tip is to label each pair according to its use or to simply purchase scissors with different colored handles.

Ironing Board

Just like the sewing machine, the ironing board does not have to be a really expensive piece of equipment. Beginners can simply use the ironing board that they may already have at home. However, expert quilters often complain that the shape of regular ironing boards does not match their needs in terms of ironing quilt materials. This is why most quilters either purchase a big board or have their existing boards customized accordingly.

The ironing boards that best suit the quilting process are often wider than regular boards. The width is also consistent from one end to another, which gives the board a wider rectangular shape as compared to regular boards. Pair this board up with a weighty steam-producing iron.

Other essential supplies that you will need for quilting include several spools of thread, a seam ripper, as well as some pins and needles.

Rotary Cutters

Some beginners may ask why a cutter is still necessary if they already have fabric scissors at hand. But do note that rotary cutters perform a slightly different function than scissors. Scissors are great for use in cutting curved patterns on any type of fabric, as well as for trimming and snipping. However, it is faster to use a rotary cutter for cutting up the straight patterns on the square pieces of fabric for quilting. This is especially beneficial for cutting an entire length of fabric in one straight line.

Choosing the right type of rotary cutter may baffle some beginners. This is why most beginners end up buying rotary cutters in a variety of sizes. But for those who are on a tight budget, buying multiple cutters wouldn't be too practical. In this case, they can settle with a rotary cutter that has a 45-millimeter blade. Most expert quilters consider this to be just the right size for cutting quilt fabric. Beginners don't have to worry about cutting the quilt layers separately, even if they would eventually end up with the same size and on the same side of the stitch.

The 45mm-blade rotary cutter is capable of cutting through at least 2 to 3 layers of fabric, including the batting. Of course, using a rotary cutter also entails having a cutting mat. This ensures that the surface of the tables and floors wouldn't be damaged. A ruler is also a must-have partner of the rotary cutter to ensure that the cut is straight and flawless. It is best to choose rulers that are specially-designed for quilting. These rulers come in different sizes and are designed to aid in cutting different lengths of the quilting fabric. Buying rulers in every size is considered as a good investment by most expert quilters.

Cutting Mat

The cutting mat is usually 18 inches by 24 inches and must be pre-marked so that it will be easier for you to cut squares. Some quilters prefer to eyeball this process, but for beginners, I highly recommend getting a mat. You can use this as a makeshift cutting board for cloth, which is magical to use if you are using the rotary cutter. There are some bigger boards, and depending on your needs, you may want to consider purchasing a table-wide board. But for starters, the standard size mentioned above can do the job.

Bias Tape Marker

A helpful tool to have is a two-inch bias tape marker, which can help you in marking the fabric for cutting. Don't use a marker in pre-cutting your fabric as the ink could bleed and even damage the fabric. Rather, always use the bias tape for your marking needs.

Thread

Two types of threads are ideal to use in quilting: white cotton and clear nylon. These threads can be used to seal up edges, attach different pieces of fabric patterns to your quilt, or work with corners. Be sure always to have thread when quilting. These thread types are ideal if you are making a quilt with bright colors, and you need something that is strong but is not that visible.

Fabric

Even though the fabric you choose entirely depends on your preference, I highly recommend getting some cotton fabric. Cotton is a natural fabric to work with, soft and wears really well. In addition, it becomes softer as you wash it, which you can't achieve with other types of fabric. Also, most fabrics have the tendency to fray once cut, but cotton is the best option for delicate patterns and designs.

Seam Ripper

Although sharp scissors could do the job, it is also ideal for getting yourself a seam ripper. This tool is used to unpick stitches. It comes with a curved blade with a sharp point end, while the opposite edge features a small ball that protects the adjacent fabric from damages. Seam rippers are available in different sizes from 1.75 inches to 6 inches. They are also available in different handle styles and colors.

Once you've got all the tools ready, it is now time to move on to the quilt's design.

CHAPTER 3:

Quilting Stitches

Herringbone Stitch

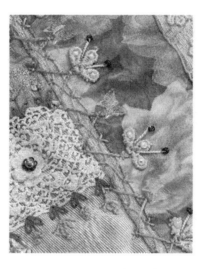

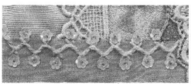

Herringbone stitch laced with contrasting thread

Herringbone is another versatile and much-loved stitch used by crazy quilters. It is a highly decorative stitch, particularly if you experiment with the spacing.

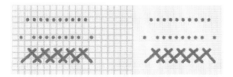

The dot pattern for basic herringbone stitch, is based on seven-count plastic canvas as a guide. The herringbone stitch is worked along two imaginary horizontal lines.

1. Bring the thread up from the back of the fabric on the lower imaginary line. Make a small stitch on the top line.

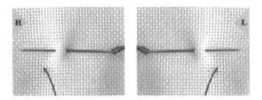

2. Pull the thread through. Take the needle diagonally and insert it on the lower line; make a small stitch.

3. Pull the thread through. Take the needle diagonally and insert it on the top line; make a small stitch.

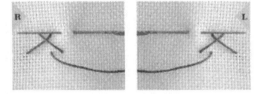

4. Repeat this process along the line.

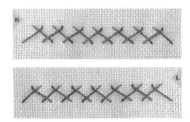 

Decorate using a combination of motif stitches: little floral motifs of French knots and detached chain stitch leaves.

Create a wider decorative seam by using slightly taller motifs. The flowers are created with motif stitches such as detached chain stitches, French knots, and quarter–buttonhole wheels. When mixing motifs, make sure the seam you are decorating is long enough to repeat each motif along the seam at least twice. If there is no repeat, there is no pattern, and it will not have the same effect. Patterns and repeats help tie a block together.

Decorate two foundation rows of herringbone back to back with small motifs—in this case, three detached chain stitches with a seed bead or French knot at the base.

Work two foundation rows slightly apart to add space for a secondary line of stitches.

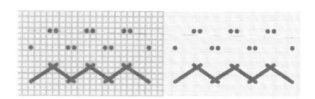

This dot pattern has been stretched to create more space to add decorative elements from the motif stitches.

Extra space allows you to mix motifs. Space will enable you to create a decorative line of hand embroidery that has a light and airy feel.

Add triangle motifs to fit the shape of the spaces.

Decorate the edges of two foundation rows of the herringbone stitch with a line of small motifs. Since the foundation row is stretched to provide more space, the seam decoration has a light and lacy feeling. This pattern would complement a block with a lot of lace or perhaps a spring theme.

Add more space for more ornate motifs and decorations by working two lines of herringbone stitches further apart.

There is sufficient space for small floral sprays, such as bullion rose garlands.

You could also utilize this space by adding some silk ribbon embroidery, larger beads, charms, or a line of buttons.

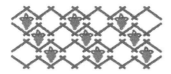

Four lines of herringbone stitch fill a space and look like a trellis. Bunches of grapes can be created using French knots or beads with small detached chain stitches for leaves.

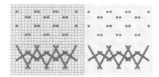

The dot pattern to create two rows of differently spaced and sized herringbone stitches worked on top of each other.

Place a motif above every second cross of the smaller line of herringbone stitches or over every cross. Or create another pattern by placing a motif over every third cross.

Add beads, sequins, and small motifs, setting up a secondary pattern in the spaces.

Build a wider design by adding motifs to the larger line of herringbone stitches.

Work four foundation lines to produce a complex pattern along a seam. A visually rich seam such as this can balance your composition.

Working two separate lines of double herringbone stitches allows for embroidered motifs to be worked between them.

Beaded Herringbone

Beaded herringbone is another variety that makes an ideal stitch to use in crazy quilting. You can use it in conjunction with the dot patterns I have suggested for the herringbone stitch or you can develop your patterns. Tip: You can also use beaded herringbone stitches over a satin ribbon. Dealing with a satin ribbon and beads on a slippery fabric is not an easy task, but it is easier if you secure the ribbon with small slip stitches. They do not have to be too perfect, because most of them will be covered with beading, and the beads are what people will notice. Just try to keep the stitches small, so the ribbon is secured and the stitches are not too noticeable.

1. Bring the thread up from the back of the fabric on the bottom left-hand side of the line. Take the needle diagonally and make a small stitch on the top line.

2. Pull the thread through.

3. Measure your seed beads against the stitch you just made to decide how many you need. Add the required number of seed beads to your thread.

4. Take the needle diagonally and insert on the lower line; make a small stitch.

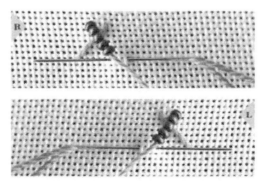

5. Pull the thread through. Take the needle diagonally and insert it on the top line; make a small stitch. Pull the thread through.

6. Add seed beads to your thread and repeat this process along the line.

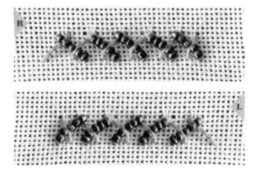

Laced Herringbone

One way to enhance an embroidery stitch quickly and easily is to lace it with a contrasting thread or ribbon. Choose any of the wonderful novelty threads and yarns, a metallic thread, or even an elegant ribbon. The possibilities are endless. The herringbone stitch is easily and quickly laced. The technique is the same as for lacing the chevron stitch or the Cretan stitch. Laced herringbone stitches can be used with the dot patterns for the herringbone stitch. Two lines of laced herringbone worked face to face are a very effective seam decoration.

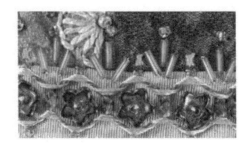

Two lines of laced herringbone stitches placed face to face

1. Work a row of herringbone stitches loosely, because the lacing will tighten the stitches slightly.

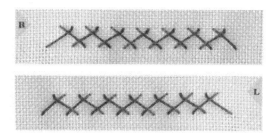

2. Bring the thread up from the back of the fabric on the lower line at the base of the first stitch. Pass the needle under the herringbone crossbar in an upward direction.

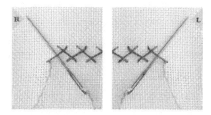

3. Move across the crossbar, turn the needle, and pass it under the next bar in a downward direction.

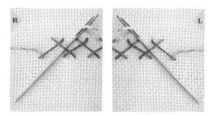

4. Move across the crossbar, turn the needle, and pass it under the next bar in an upward direction.

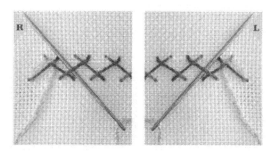

5. Work along with the herringbone stitches, keeping the lacing thread slightly loose to avoid distorting the fabric.

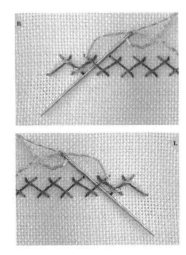

6. Continue lacing until you reach the end of the line.

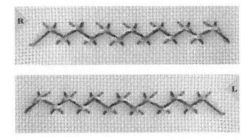

Tied Herringbone

The tied herringbone is another versatile stitch that is quick and easy to work, yet it adds something extra to a line of plain herringbone stitches. You can tie a herringbone stitch in a variety of ways. Choose the one that suits your project.

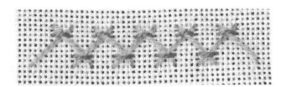

Herringbone stitch tied where the bars cross, usually using a straight stitch. Use any of the dot patterns for herringbone stitch and further enhance them by adding a few stitches.

Herringbone stitch tied with an upright cross-stitch. Herringbone stitches can be tied with a French knot, various cross-stitches, bullion knots, sequins, seed beads, or bugle beads.

Herringbone stitch tied with a detached chain stitch

Herringbone stitch tied with a straight stitch and decorated with small motifs and beads

Feather Stitch

The feather stitch is one of the most popular foundation stitches because of its versatility. You can work it along a seam or let it meander across a block. Its organic feel is ideal for floral sprays; you can add many additional decorative stitches to the spines, or tuck beads and stitches in the fork of the spines. Not only it is pretty but also quick to work!

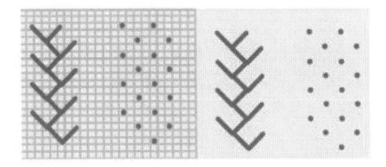

The dot pattern for the basic feather stitch using seven-count plastic canvas as a guide (refer to Marking Your Fabric).

Once you master the stitch, you can work it in a free-form, organic manner.

1. Bring the thread up from the back of the fabric at the top of where you want to create the stitch.

Insert the needle next to and even with the point where the thread emerged, and come up below and between the 2 points, looping the working thread under the needle.

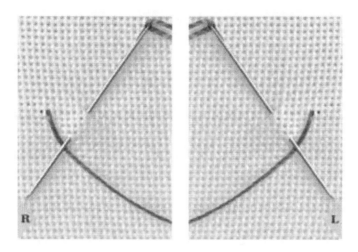

2. Pull the thread; it should make a V. Insert the needle on the other side, next to and even with the point where the thread emerged, and come up below and between the 2 points, looping the working thread under the needle.

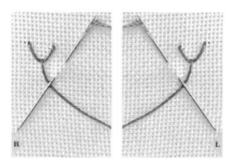

3. Repeat this process.

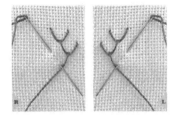

4. Work these stitches, alternating from side to side.

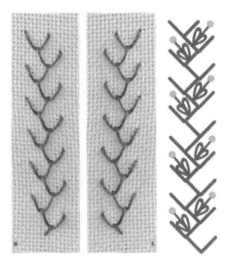

Add small floral motifs or beads to the fork of each stitch. I have illustrated detached chain stitches and French knots, but as with all these patterns, you can use any of the motif stitches with sequins or beads.

Add decorative motifs to the tip of each arm.

Creating a secondary pattern along the stitch is easy. Establish a line of motifs or beads tucked in the forks, and then add a second pattern to the arms. Combine small motifs, such as a grouping of French knots and detached chain leaves spaced along every second arm of the feather-stitch line.

Stitch a sequin or bead to the base of each fork to create another type of pattern.

Bugle beads tucked into the fork of a feather stitch

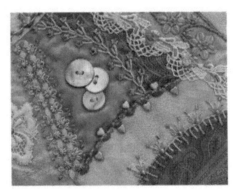

Feather stitch decorated with metal novelty beads and bugle beads

Beaded feather stitch

Bullion knots tucked into the fork of a feather stitch

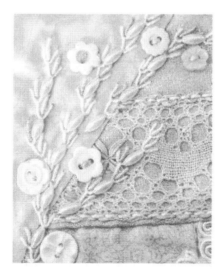

The beaded feather stitch lends itself to incorporating larger beads and bugle beads.

Leaf Stitch

Leaf stitches tucked into the fork of feather stitches and worked alongside fargo roses and detached chain stitches

Use this stitch for flowers, buds, and leaves. Here, little bud-like motifs appear at the end of a curve of stem stitches.

This stitch is also known as the Japanese ribbon stitch. Quick and easy to work, the ribbon folds in on itself during the process of stitching, creating the leaf.

1. Bring the ribbon up from the back of the fabric and lay the ribbon against the fabric (untwisted and flat). Hold the ribbon flat but not too tight, place the tip of the needle into the center of the ribbon.

2. Gently pull the needle through the ribbon and the fabric. Pull until the ribbon folds back on itself and forms a leaf shape. Don't pull too tight! If you do, the fold will tighten and go straight through the fabric. Keep your stitches loose for a natural look.

3. Repeat the process as needed.

Leaf Stitch Flowers

Silk ribbon daisies mixed with woven ribbon roses and novelty beads

Silk ribbon daisies with French knot centers on a seam

5-, 6-, and 8-petal flowers are quick and easy using the leaf stitch. I used a 7 mm ribbon to demonstrate an 8-petal flower.

1. Mark the fabric for the middle of the flower and the petal points.

2. Bring the ribbon to the front of the fabric and work the first leaf stitch (See Leaf Stitch, Steps 1 and 2).

3. Work leaf stitches at 3 o'clock, 6 o'clock, and 9 o'clock.

4. Work a leaf stitch between the stitches created in Step 3.

5. Add a bead in the center and you have a flower!

CHAPTER 4:

Quilting Patterns

Traditionally, the quilt block forms the whole design on top of a quilt, which is a design of quilt fabric with an alternative or repeated plain blocks. Those quilt blocks are in a variety of sizes, but all blocks that will be used at the single top will be in the same size.

The Nine-Plot Patterns

Usually, in the traditional piece of the quilt block, there's a lot of variations, but this commonly consists of geometric shapes that are sewn together to form a square which is usually "8 or 16" in sizes.

One of the most popular patterns is the Nine-Plot Pattern. This is made by sewing the patches or five patterned pieces to the four-square pieces in an alternate order. In this, the nine sewn squares create one block.

The Churn Dashboard

This is one variation that is done by quilting one piece of a square divided into two balanced rectangles considering the basics of the Nine-Plot pattern. This pattern associates the various rectangle and triangles to distend the nine-plot pattern.

The Shoo Get Away Fly Pattern

There can be one possible design when the squares in the nine-plot pattern are created through the use of two triangles. It is the Shoo Get Away Fly pattern. It varies from the Nine-Plot Pattern by the division of the four pieces of corner fabric into the light and dark triangles.

Extensive Tract Queen Pattern

In each unit of the block, there are always different scales used. This pattern combines two large triangles in the surface units and in the middle units four squares. On its center unit, there is one full-size square. Each unit has equal measurement and fits together. These three patterns are all variations created from the Nine Plot Pattern and will be your guide to deal with more complex blocks or patterns.

CHAPTER 5:

Quilting Techniques

Described below, you will find exciting techniques you certainly would love to try. You may find that one method could help you to achieve the look you are seeking for in one quilt, while another gives you the right appearance.

Piecing

Even the simplest patchwork quilts are pieced, so this could be the first technique to experience. Piecing is simple, and you can do it by hand or using a machine.

What you'll need:

- A fabric of your choice
- Cardboard
- Scissors
- Ruler or measuring tape
- Rotary cutter and mat
- Pins
- Needle and thread or sewing machine

What you'll do:

1. Determine your pattern. Quilt patterns are made up not only of individual pieces but also of the colors that you'll use to bring them alive. Take the time to lay pieces of fabric next to one another so you can see how they'll look in the finished piece.

2. Transfer your pattern onto pieces of cardboard. For example, if you're making a Nine Patch, you'll cut out a single square of cardboard that matches the size of the squares you want to make. If you're making an Irish Chain, you'll cut two sizes of squares, etc. Your template needs to be slightly bigger than the pieces themself because you need what is called a seam allowance. So, make each piece about ¼-inch larger all the way around.

3. Use your cardboard template to cut out your fabric. Remember to keep the overall pattern and colors in mind as you go.

4. Begin to piece your first block by joining the individual pieces of fabric together using pins on the backside of the fabric. You have ¼-inch of seam allowance on each side to play with; measure and use it so that you'll have plenty of room to sew.

5. Once you have a block pinned together, sew up your seams.

6. After you've completed the necessary number of blocks for the quilt, stitch each block together. Pay attention to the direction they face so that your pattern will show up when the quilt is finished.

Backing And Binding

Once you've finished piecing your blocks together, what you will have is a quilt top. Your top needs to be backed and bound together so that you can complete it. Backing refers to the single piece of fabric that will go on the underside of the quilt. You can use anything from an old sheet to a second quilt top, but many people prefer to use a solid color that coordinates with the colors on the top of the quilt. Between the two layers, you'll place a layer of batting. This is the insulation that gives the quilt its warmth. If you are planning on making a light summer quilt, batting is not necessary. For warm, winter quilts, you may want to use a very thick layer in the center to give it extra weight.

The binding is the edge of the quilt. It hides the unfinished edges of the top and the batting in the center. Binding can be made of anything, but most people use fabric or fabric tape that is cut on a bias. This helps to give strength and lack of stretch necessary to hold everything together. You can find bias tape ready-made at most craft or fabric shops, or you can cut your own from fabric you have in the house.

To back and bind your quilt, you could think about it as a quilt sandwich:

1. Place your backing fabric face down, then layer the batting on top, and finally, your quilt top faces up.

2. Pull everything smooth and taut to get out the wrinkles. Some people at this stage prefer to baste the three layers together with big, loose stitches that you'll remove later. These loose stitches hold everything in place until you have finished, and bind after quilting or tying. Other people prefer to bind immediately and let the binding hold everything together.

3. When you're ready to bind, pin the binding over the edges of the quilt, making sure it's even on both sides. Now stitch the binding down through the three layers either by hand or on a machine, trying to get as close to the edge of the binding as you can get without causing gaps.

Tying

Tying is the simplest way to hold your quilt sandwich together, and it's often the first technique most people learn. You can use anything to tie your quilt, but most people prefer yarn as it holds securely and can come in so many different colors.

What you'll need:

- Yarn of your choice
- Large embroidery needle

What you'll do:

1. Take a look at your quilt. You'll want to find the best places to tie so that your ties are evenly spaced across the design.

If you're using large blocks, you can put your ties in the corners.

If you're making a patchwork quilt, you can count out a few blocks and tie the corners of every three or four – whatever will give you the most balanced look.

2. Thread the yarn through the embroidery needle, but don't tie off the ends.

3. Poke the needle down through the top of your quilt through to the other side where you determined the tie should be.

4. Pull the needle all the way through so that the yarn stays about 2-inches above the quilt top.

5. Grasp one of the two ends of the yarn on top of the quilt to hold it in place, pull the needle and the other end all the way through.

6. Poke the needle back up through the quilt from the bottom, pulling the rest of the yarn with it so that you have two ends coming up through the top of the quilt.

7. Trim the second end so that it matches the length of the first and tie to the two pieces of yarn into a square knot on the top of the quilt.

8. Repeat for the rest of the areas you plan on tying.

Stitching in the Ditch

When you first begin to hand quilt and stitch your three layers together for the first time, it will take you a little while to get used to the rocking stitches and to keep the length and size of your stitches even. Therefore, you need a way to practice that doesn't require you also to follow a pattern of stitches, and that can help disguise the uneven nature of your work until it improves. One of the best ways to do this is to stitch in the ditch. Stitching in the ditch means that you'll follow the outline of each one of your quilt pieces, putting your quilting stitches in the "ditch" that the seams make between two pieces. When complete, the stitches give your quilt the dimension and depth it needs and holds everything together well, but you won't see the stitches unless you go looking for them. This is a great method of hiding your mistakes as a beginner. Don't worry though; by the time you've quilted an entire top, your stitches will become good enough to begin putting them out in the open where they can be seen.

Hand Quilting

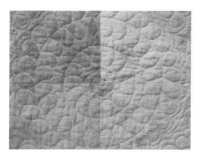

Whether you plan to stitch in the ditch or you want to make your stitches more noticeable, the technique is basically the same. This type of stitching is a little different than what you might be used to already, simply because you'll never see the underside of your stitching as you go; you have to work by touch.

What you'll need:

- Thimble
- Quilt frame
- Quilting needle
- Thread

What you'll do:

1. Set up your quilt on the frame so that you have the unit you intend to work on pulled taut and easily accessible.

2. Thread your needle and tie a knot at the end of the thread.

3. Push the needle up through the quilt from the bottom. Once the knot has reached the fabric, give your needle a short, fast tug. The idea is to pop your knot through your backing into the middle of the quilt where it won't be seen. Don't worry if you have to try this a few times, or if you keep popping through all three layers at once, this takes a lot of practice to get right and you more than likely won't on the first try.

4. Once the knot is in the center, push the tip of the needle down through the three layers. With your finger covered in a thimble, feel for the tip of the needle and push it right back up through the quilt to the top a little way from where it just came through. Do not pull your needle all the way through yet.

5. When your needle shows through the top of the quilt, guide it forward and down again. The idea is to gather roughly 4 stitches on your needle at once before you pull the thread all the way through. When you're doing it correctly, it will feel like you're rocking the needle through the quilt, up and down, back and forth. It's very rhythmic, and once you get going, you'll be able to quilt for a while without tiring.

Your finger on the hand on top of the quilt will eventually callus and toughen up, but you may find that it gets pretty sore during the first couple of days of quilting.

Once you've gotten the hang of the stitches, you can try making them appear as part of the quilt pattern. Start with straight lines, going across or diagonally through your blocks. Then try making simple shapes like circles in large units of fabric. Eventually, you can begin stitching patterns and complex designs into the quilt surface.

Machine Quilting

Machine quilting is a very different animal than hand quilting or sewing on your standard sewing machine. However, it's very fast and easy, and you can usually get the hang of it pretty quickly.

Quilting machines are huge affairs with a frame attached on rollers so you can pull your quilt onto it, then quilt it unit by unit by moving it along the rollers. You'll control the arms of the machine and the pattern you use to quilt with by hand controls; moving your hands will move the arms and guide the needles over your quilt.

If you try machine quilting, you may want to start with some simple patterns or shapes, or just stitch in the ditch your first time until you get used to how it works. From there, you can quickly begin a variety of other patterns. Some quilters believe that machine quilting is cheating or not a true method of quilting, but if you want to finish it quickly, this can definitely get the job done fast.

CHAPTER 6:

How to Choose Color, Fabric and Pattern?

Once you have finalized the design, you have a fair idea of what you want to make and how you expect it to look. Therefore, the next thing that you need to do is to pick a pattern for your quilt. After you are done with this, you will need to finalize the type, color and nature of fabrics that you wish to use for your quilt.

Choosing the Fabric

When it comes to choosing the fabric for creating your quilt, the most important facet of the fabric you need to pay attention to is the purpose you are creating the quilt for. This is perhaps the reason why you will notice an excessive use of cotton and cotton-mixes in quilt making. The versatility, strength, anti-allergic and non-flammable characteristics of this fabric are the fundamental reasons why cotton and its mixes make a good quilting fabric.

If you have chosen a colorful pattern that requires a bright foundation fabric, you are likely to be tempted by synthetic fabrics. However, before you decide to pick them, be sure to understand these fabrics crease much more and are extremely difficult to quilt, particularly because you are still a beginner. Therefore, for now, using cotton is recommended. Once you gain experience, working with spongy fabrics as synthetics may also become easier for you.

If you are using a colored fabric, ensure the colors are fast and will not bleed when washed. In addition, do not use a 'too heavy' or 'too light' fabric. Fabrics that are too heavy, like denim, is extremely difficult to quilt. Similarly, fabrics like organza are too flimsy for quilting and do not make a good fit for this purpose.

Choosing Color of The Foundation Fabric

Regardless of whether you are choosing the color of the foundation fabric or the pattern you plan to put in the quilt blocks, the most important thing you need to consider is the mood and purpose of the quilt concerned.

Most people who create a quilt for a friend or loved one generally try to use something of sentimental value to the receiver of the gift in the quilt. For example, they may use a patch from their favorite old dress or granny's handkerchief, adding an element of thoughtfulness to the quilt.

While choosing colors, also remember that some colors like yellows and reds are warm. These colors are appropriate for use in lounges as they tend to add alertness and activity to the aura of the room. On the other hand, colors like greens and browns are cool colors. These colors are used in bedrooms or rooms meant for resting.

Cutting And Designing Templates

Now that you have the raw materials ready, and you are all set to start quilting, you need to design your templates. If you plan to create a quilt that is just made of squares, then you will not need any templates. All you need to do is use the rotary board and cutter to get perfect squares from your fabric. This is also true for patchwork designs.

On the other hand, if you plan to create a quilt with applique designs with different shapes, you will need to cut out templates for the shapes you intend to use. For cutting out the templates, you will again need the rotary cutter and board. However, ensure you use different rotary cutters for fabric and template boards for the simple reason that using cutters on hard surfaces like boards blunts the blade. You may use any of the different applique techniques for transferring designs from the template to the fabric.

Marking and cutting the fabric is one of the steps you have to take since you cannot afford to make mistakes as a result of the sheer criticality of the step. If you make any mistakes in marking or cutting the fabric, the overall appearance of the quilt will be significantly impacted. First things first, you need to get the right fabric marker for yourself.

Testing the fabric marker before actually using it on your fabric for marking your design is highly recommended. In order to test your fabric marker, you can cut out a corner of the fabric that you intend to use for your quilt. Next, make marks on this test fabric. These marks must be similar to the marks you will be making in your actual design.

You can use the pattern shown above to cut your fabric. Even though 2, 4, 9 and 11 are the same size, do not interchange their position for the simple reason that no matter how perfectly you cut them out, they will fit perfectly only in the places from which and for which they have been cut. Also, cut the vertical pieces for 4 and 9, while you cut horizontal pieces for 2 and 11. Several other patterns can be used. The pattern shown above has been kept here for its sheer simplicity.

Whenever you choose the fabric for creating templates, be sure to use the exact fabric. Using scrap fabric for the templates will not help you visualize the final product so well. Besides this, washing the sample fabric will also tell if the marker tags will go away or not. If you use a different fabric, you will not be able to estimate this facet accurately.

Lastly, remember to use sharp scissors for cutting out the templates. Blunt scissors usually tear off the edges spoiling the fabric shape completely. Keep the blocks in order so it will be easier for you to assemble your quilt as described in the next unit.

CHAPTER 7:

Influence of Function And Style

Influence of Function

Before selecting any fabrics or embellishments, there should be some type of plan, whether it is written or not. Function plays a huge role in what is created. It answers the questions: What types of fabrics should I use? Do the threads and other embellishments need to be color-fast so the item can be laundered? Will the item be handled a lot?

For example, let's say we want to make a purse. How we plan on using that purse is critical to the very basic decisions we should be making about our fabrics and embellishments. Will the purse be an every-day type and require laundry in the future? If so, the fabrics need to be resistant to shrinkage, colorfast, and durable enough to withstand the water. The fabrics and embellishments should be able to tolerate the agitation of the washer or by hand. Will it need to be air-dried or in a machine? If in a machine, the embellishments would need to withstand heat without melting.

The "answers" to your contemplation about Function...can determine how much embellishing you decide to include on your project, the materials chosen to use in that embellishment phase, and even the fabrics selected to piece the crazy quilt item in the beginning.

So, begin all projects with the question "What is the Function" of this item. Once this is decided, you can start thinking about a theme (or no theme); and a color palette for fabrics and embellishments. If you are making items for other individuals, you also need to consider any allergies to certain fibers when creating the item. Some wools, linens, or synthetics might not be good choices for "saleable" items.

Influence of Style

When we think of crazy quilts, we automatically get a vision of Victorian Style work with lovely embroidery on the seams and an occasional motif in the patches. This is not the only style made today. Most people are drawn to one style of creation over the others, but all have their uses. The type of blocks created also can differ depending on the method chosen.

Victorian Style work uses opulent fabrics for the basic block. Satin, silks, brocades, and fine quality types of cotton are all acceptable to produce this style. Delicate embroidery work with minimal motifs that are traditional of this style. The main visual element is the seam embroidery and fabrics used.

Utilitarian Style work has minimal or no motifs, relying on the embroidery of the seams to provide the viewer with a visual repose from the commonly used fabrics of cotton, wool, linen, etc. found in the household's closets perhaps. These are quilts than can be washed and used daily.

Crafty Style work is like the original 1800's style on steroids. Today, we are fortunate to have machine-made laces, trims, ribbons, fancy fibers, threads, and the list goes on and on! Our Victorian sisters would be envious for sure! This style has no limits and no boundaries...judging from the present displays of plastic baubles and dismantled silk flowers adorning many projects in books and magazines today. These have a few embroidery motifs but include many ready-made embellishments.

Shabby Chic Style layers lace over and over itself to create a foundation, often so much that the fabrics creating the block can hardly be seen. These are covered in beautiful beading, silk ribbon flowers and lovely embroidery seams, but have few embroidery motifs present. The key visual element is lace.

The jewelry style is one that has more beading than anything else. Everywhere you look you will see beads.

A statement in B-L-I-N-G!

Modern Style includes an element of Crafty Style but is more reserved in the number of things and the quality of embellishments does not include plastics or many readymade items. The blocks can contain some lace and trims but not so that they define a style of their own.

Storybook Style primarily ignores the boundaries of seams and patches thinking, using the patchwork only as a blank surface for telling a story. This style is heavy in motifs but may have few or no embroidered seams.

Landscape Style is similar to the Storybook Style but it deals only in nature scenes of rolling hills, wooded venues, or watery depths. Under the Sea is a favorite theme of this style of work.

Textural Style contains almost total surface coverage with embroidery work. The stitching includes many raised stitches to add texture similar to a topography map including mountains and valleys.

Styles are created only by the limits of our imagination.

CHAPTER 8:

Caring for Your Quilt

Making a quilt takes a lot of time and you should spend many days giving your utmost care and attention to create your masterpiece. It is crucial to understand how to take care of your quilt so that you can keep it for as long as you want. Taking care of your quilt is very important and unlike other materials that are mass-produced in factories, handmade quilts are very delicate.

Washing Quilt

If you use your quilt daily, it will get dirty pretty fast. It is essential to you wash your quilt regularly. Most laundry detergents are safe for all types of quilts. Quilts do not have any special washing instructions. You can even use a dryer once you finish washing the quilt. However, if you are using delicate fabrics, you need to dry it in the air. Avoid direct sunlight as much as possible because it may result in color fading. You also have the option to hand wash the quilt, especially if the quilt is made from sensitive fabrics that are not cotton. When washing quilts by hand, use a large bathtub and make sure that the detergent is dissolved well.

Storing a Quilt

Storing a small quilt is very easy but if you have completed a large quilt, you need to know how to store your quilt. The right way of storing the quilt can lengthen the lifespan of the quilt. Below are tips on how to store quilts properly.

• Store the quilts in a dry place that has good air circulation. The presence of moisture can attract the growth of mold and mildew that can destroy the fibers of the quilt fabric.

• Wrap your quilt in a cotton sheet and never store them inside a plastic box. Using a non-breathable material can cause moisture build-up that can encourage the growth of molds and mildew.

• Avoid storing them in places that are extremely hot or cold. The change i temperature can cause stress to the fabric thus making it easily deteriorate after a few years.

• Do not let bugs and mice near your quilt. Insects and mice tend to damage the fabric by eating the fibers or making a nest out of them.

• If you do not have enough storage space for your quilts, you can always roll them. Rolling them removes creases that can damage the quality of your quilt.

Pressing the Quilt

Ironing the quilt is essential to remove creases and to give a flawless look. Below are the tips on how to press or iron the quilt.

• Some materials are sensitive to heat; thus it is important to use the right heat settings when pressing the quilt. Cotton can endure high heat but if the quilt is made from polyester or silk, then you need to use a lower heat setting to prevent burning the fabric.

• Dry ironing the quilt is the preferred way of pressing the quilt. Do not steam iron because the moisture from the steam can be trapped in the batting that can cause damping, which encourages the growth of mildew and mold.

• Take extra care if you are pressing appliqué quilts because it may cause the embroidery thread to burn.

• Consider the age as well as the condition of your quilt. If your quilt is of a vintage quality, then get professional cleaning services to clean your quilt because the threads may integrate anytime when handled incorrectly.

CHAPTER 9:

Common Beginner Mistakes and Ways to Avoid Them

Despite the individuality of each person, there are always patterns in behavior that make it almost inevitable for inexperienced people – even you – to commit commonly made neophyte mistakes. These are mainly influenced by the way you utilize your quilt-making skills in completing a project. Most of these mistakes involve accuracy, which is usually deterred by impatience. Here are some of the most common activities or practices that make the quilter prone to committing errors as he or she works:

Combining Prewashed and Unwashed Cloths Together

There has been a constant debate in the quilting community on whether you should prewash the fabric or not. The majority prefers to leave the textile as it is because washing causes most cloths to shrink – some to a greater degree than others. Nevertheless, it all boils down to personal preference.

Inexperienced quilters may be unaware of the slight shrinkage some washed pieces of cloth undergo and may think that it is alright to combine these with unwashed fabrics.

However, once you have the piece laundered for the first time after completion of the project, you may notice a slight distortion in the patches. Unless you are aiming for a slightly puckered look, do not mix them.

Sewing Too Hastily

You may only have a short time to work on a project or perhaps you are excited to see the finished product but do it quickly is not the solution. Making haste sacrifices the uniformity of your stitches and the overall quality of your work. Slow down and be patient. Doing so will improve your accuracy and decrease the margin for error. You can gradually increase your pace once you get the hang of quilting. Most sewing machines are designed with adjustable speed settings. Take advantage of this and set it to a slower speed.

Beginning with A Complex Quilt Pattern

Some beginners may fail to understand the meticulous nature of quilting. Or perhaps they feel mighty confident of their skills that they decide to work on a complex design as their first project. Sometimes, when they fail to come up with the desired output or are having a hard time completing the pattern, they become overwhelmed with frustration and quit.

It is important to take baby steps when starting. You should be well aware of your limitations as a beginner and commence with a simple pattern. There are a lot of stunning and simple designs you could work on – all you need are the right resources. If you look close enough at the bone structure of some contemporary yet simple designs, you will notice that the secret to their beauty is in the sewing of pieces of cloth in non-traditional arrangements.

Pressing the Fabric Too Hard or Too Timidly

Pressing is a delicate procedure that may either make or break your patchwork. It is not as simple as ironing out clothes as you have to be slightly more sensitive to the length of time by which you press the pieces of cloth. Moreover, you do not move the iron back and forth on the patches – similar to the way you iron clothes. To press quilting fabric, you have to lay the iron on top of the patchwork, without any sort of movement whatsoever, and wait until the cloth has been adequately heated up. This is to prevent the quilting cloth from getting stretched out.

Most beginners have a slight difficulty in estimating the amount of time they can press the fabric. Many quit the procedure prematurely due to the fear of burning the cloth.

CHAPTER 10:

Quilting Tips and Tricks

L ike every trade, quilting has many tips and tricks that can help make quilting easier for you. To start, if you follow these tricks you will have fewer flaws even on your first quilt. The more you quilt and practice, the easier quilting will become and the more tricks you will come up with on your own. Each of the following tips can be used depending on your creativity and working style.

Trick # 1 Pre-wound Bobbins:

To make the sewing process easier you can buy pre-wound bobbins or if you have extra time to wind them yourself, do that and keep them in a designated case. That way, they are always available for your use and you can quickly find them before a project begins and throughout the process.

Trick #2 Seam Allowance Accuracy:

You should always be sewing with a 1/4 "seam allowance. If you are doing a lot of quilting and not much else, you should keep your machine in this setting. Otherwise, have a small piece of test fabric next to your sewing machine and always do an accuracy test before you begin a project. This will help to reduce surprises after you start sewing.

Trick #3 Caring for Your Machine:

Your sewing machine is an expensive tool. It is the heart and soul of your quilting and you should take care of it as you would anything else that you value. Maintaining your machine will ensure that your projects do not get interrupted or, worse, not be able to get going at all, because of mechanical failures and the like. After each project, it is essential to clean and take out all the excess threads and fabrics. Based on how often you use your sewing machine and what type of machine it is, you may also need to oil it regularly. If your sewing machine manual does not include instructions on oiling, then it has been pre-lubricated at the factory and will not require additional lubrication. If you have lost your manual or are still unsure, bring your sewing machine into any quilt shop and they will be able to help you.

Further sewing machine maintenance tips:

Be sure to constantly turn the hand-wheel towards you in a counter-clockwise direction. If you turn the hand-wheel in the other direction, not facing you, it may not get the right timing. This will cause premature wear and tear and expensive repairs from a service center.

Before sewing, check your presser foot if the position is downwards. Your thread will jumble and your bobbin will jam if you sew with the presser foot in the upward position.

Always change your needles. After using your needles for 16 hours, they will become dull and weak. This can damage your fabric as well as your machine. Your sewing machine may require only changing parts of its brand. Be sure to read your instruction manual to find out more.

Always use the correct bobbin on your machine. Many bobbins such as Class 66, Class 15 and Class 15J bobbins look extremely similar. However, by using an incorrect bobbin class in your machine, you can cause a great deal of damage and breakage to your sewing machine.

Trick #4 Watch Out for Pins:

Pins are extremely helpful and you will have the opportunity to use them a lot for every quilting project. However, be careful because things can get messy if you sew over them. Indeed you could easily break a needle and damage your sewing machine or worse, break into your hands or jump into your eyes. Not to mention it is just a pain to get them out of the fabric once you have sewn them into your piece. To avoid this catastrophe remove them just before you sew over the fabric.

Trick #5 Working with Large Quilts:

Once you have done a few small projects you may feel compelled to do a large quilt. Great Just keep in mind that large quilts are very heavy and can be cumbersome. So much so that some large, heavy quilts can even pull down your sewing machine right off your sewing table to avoid this, work on the floor or keep your quilt rolled up on one side. This will alleviate bunching and distribute the weight a little better.

CHAPTER 11:

Project: Vintage Flowers

Faded flowers mixed with antique colors give this lovely quilt and matching cushion a wonderfully vintage feel, although the design could easily be made from brighter contemporary colors. Little birds sitting atop wooden spools with pretty flowers give texture and dimension to the design.

The sixteen-patch blocks in the quilt are made up of squares and are very straightforward to stitch. The placement of light and dark squares also creates a strong diagonal element to the quilt. The spool blocks are a charming combination of needle-turn appliqué, English paper piecing, yoyo flowers and easy stitchery, with the layout of the motifs varied over the quilt to provide added interest.

A cushion project uses the same techniques, plus a plain border decorated with hand quilting, and would be a good way to practice the techniques before beginning on the quilt.

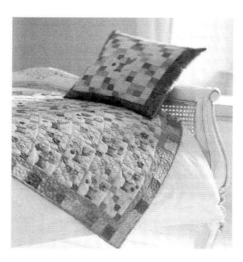

Flower Spool Quilt

This antique-style quilt uses soft and faded colors. Texture and dimension are created with English paper pieced hexagons and yoyo flowers. A fat eighth is approximately 9in × 22in (22.9cm × 56cm).

You will need…

- Cream fabric for background 1yd/m
- Twelve blue and twelve pink prints, fat eighth yd/m each
- Aged blue/grey print for appliqué birds 4in × 12in (10.2cm × 30.5cm)
- Soft brown floral for spool tops 8in × 16in (20.3cm × 40cm)
- Turquoise and blue wool for flowers 8in × 12in (20cm × 30.5cm) each
- Mauve print for inner border 6in (15.2cm) (width of fabric)
- Precut hexagons for English paper pieced flowers with 1⁄4in (6mm) sides
- Stranded embroidery cotton (floss) – (I used Cosmo threads but DMC equivalents are given in brackets): soft charcoal (413), vintage brown (611), aged fawn (648), dark antique blue (926) and light antique blue (927)
- Fabric for binding 21⁄2in (6.3cm) wide × 160in (406cm) approx.
- Backing fabric 42in × 50in (107cm × 127cm)
- Wadding (batting) 42in × 50in (107cm × 127cm)

- Fusible web

- Template plastic

- Fine-tipped fabric marking pen

- Light box (optional)

- Glue pen (optional)

- Tacking (basting) glue (optional)

Finished size:

41½in × 33½in (105.4cm × 85.1cm)

Cutting the squares

1. From cream background fabric cut thirty-one 4½in squares for the flower spool blocks and 256 1½in (3.8cm) squares for use in the sixteen-patch blocks. From the blue and pink fabrics cut a total of 256 1½in (3.8cm) squares for use in the sixteen-patch blocks (about eleven squares from each of the twenty-four fabrics).

Making the sixteen-patch blocks

2. Randomly select your 1½in (3.8cm) squares for the blocks: you need four blues (A), four pink (B) and eight cream (C). Using ¼in (6mm) seams join the squares together as in Fig 1. Make thirty-two of these blocks in total. Each finished block should be 4½in (11.4cm) square.

Fig 1

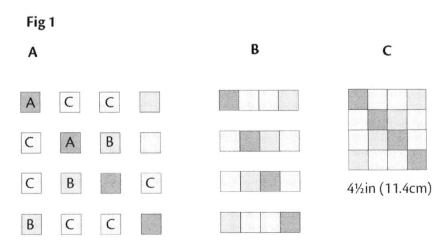

4½in (11.4cm)

Making the yoyos

3. The flower spool blocks are made of yoyos, hexagon paper-pieced flowers and appliquéd flowers, birds and spools. To make the yoyos, make a template from template plastic using the circle template supplied in Templates. From assorted blueprints make about forty-seven yoyos – see Making Yoyos in Techniques.

Making the hexagon flowers

4. Make a template from template plastic (seam allowance is already included) and use it to cut six hexagons (petals) and one hexagon (flower center) for each flower from assorted blue and pink prints.

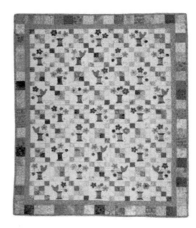

You need to make about eleven of these tiny hexagon flowers. See English Paper Piecing in the Techniques unit. Sew seven hexagons together to create a seven-piece flower.

Making the wool flowers

5. Using the turquoise and blue wool and fusible web appliqué, create the wool flowers (see Fusible Web Method in Techniques). Prepare a total of forty flowers from the two wool colors.

Working the appliqué

6. Using the templates and a needle-turn appliqué method (see Needle-turn method in Techniques), cut out and prepare the following: thirty-one spools from your assorted prints; sixty-two spool top/bottoms from the soft brown floral and the aged blue/grey print and about eleven birds. Note that some of these need to be facing right and some facing left.

Making the flower spool blocks

7. Take the thirty-one 4½in (11.4cm) cream background squares cut earlier and position the spool, bird and the various flowers on the squares. Although the same components were used in these blocks, I used a variety of arrangements within each block. Some blocks have a bird, some don't, which I think makes the quilt looks more interesting.

8. Once you have decided on the layout for each block, position the appliqué shapes and glue or pin them in place.

9. Stitch the appliqué shapes in position using blind hem stitch and thread matching the background fabric. Sew the yoyos into place and then add groups of three straight stitches in arrow shapes around the edges, about five around each yoyo, using two strands of light blue (DMC 927) embroidery thread.

10. Using a fine-tipped fabric marking pen either freehand draw or use a light box to trace the lines for the surface embroidery, i.e., the thread on the spool, stems and leaves for the flowers, beaks, wings and eyes on the birds. I used Cosmo threads but DMC equivalents have been given in the You Will Need list. Use two strands of thread for all the embroidery. Work backstitch in brown for the stems and leaves and charcoal for the thread on the spools. Fill the flower centers with French knots in dark blue. Backstitch the birds' wings in fawn. Work the running stitch on the birds' tails in light blue and the beaks in dark blue satin stitch. Stitch a French knot in light blue for the eyes.

Joining the blocks

11. Using 1⁄4in (6mm) seams join all the blocks together in rows as shown in Fig 2, alternating the sixteen-patch blocks with the flower spool blocks. Arrange the blocks, so the blue and pink colors in the sixteen-patch blocks run diagonally. Now join the rows together, pinning together carefully so the seams align.

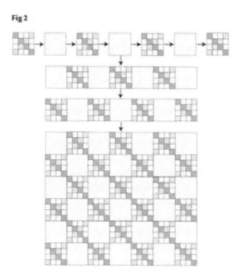

Fig 2

Tip

When sewing the blocks together push the seams in one row of blocks in a single direction and the seams in the next row of blocks in another direction. Alternating the pushing this way will help the seams nest together and lie flat when you sew all the rows together.

Adding the borders

12. For the inner border, use the mauve print and cut two strips 1½in × 28½in (3.8cm × 72.4cm) for the top and bottom borders. Sew these to the quilt top with ¼in (6mm) seams and press (Fig 3). Cut two strips 1½in × 38½in (3.8cm × 97.8cm) for the side borders. Sew these to the quilt top and press.

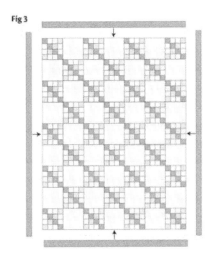

Fig 3

13. For the outer border, use assorted prints to cut seventy-two 2½in (6.3cm) squares. Select squares at random and join nineteen together. Sew to the side of the quilt and press the seam. Repeat for the other side (Fig 4). Continue selecting squares at random and join seventeen together. Sew to the bottom of the quilt and press the seam. Repeat for the top border.

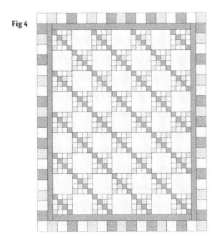

Fig 4

14. Make a quilt sandwich from the quilt top, wadding (batting) and backing and quilt as desired. I had my quilt professionally longarm quilted by Barb Cowan.

15. Prepare your binding – I used 2½in (6.3cm) wide double-fold binding but if you want wider or narrow then re-calculate your fabric requirements. Join sufficient strips to go around the quilt – at least 160in (406cm). Bind the quilt following the directions for binding.

Flower Spool Cushion

Making a cushion is a great way to practice techniques and try out fabrics before moving on to a larger quilt. This cushion has just one spool block, surrounded by eight sixteen-patch blocks.

You will need…

- *Antique cream fabric for background 10in (25.4cm)*
- Six antique blue prints/florals each 4½in (11.4cm) square
- Six antique pink prints/florals each 4½in (11.4cm) square
- Aged blue/grey print for appliquéd birds 2in (5cm) square
- Soft brown floral for spool tops 2in (5cm) square
- Antique blue wool for flower 2in (5cm) square

- Stranded embroidery cotton (floss) – (I used Cosmo threads but DMC equivalents are given in brackets): soft charcoal (413), vintage brown (611), aged fawn (648), dark antique blue (926) and light antique blue (927)
- Backing fabric 20in (51cm) square
- Fusible lightweight wadding (pellon) two pieces 16½in (42cm) square
- Toy stuffing or cushion pad
- Tacking (basting) glue (optional)

Finished size:

16in (41cm) square

Making the blocks

1. From cream background fabric, cut one 4½in square for the flower spool block. Cut the blueprints into fifty-four 1½in (3.8cm) squares. Cut the antique pink prints into fifty-four 1½in (3.8cm) squares. This makes a total of 128 squares.

2. Prepare one flower spool block and eight sixteen-patch blocks, as described in the Flower Spool Quilt. Work the embroidery as described in step 10 of the Flower Spool Quilt. Using 1/4in (6mm) seams, sew the blocks together in rows and then sew the rows together (Fig 1).

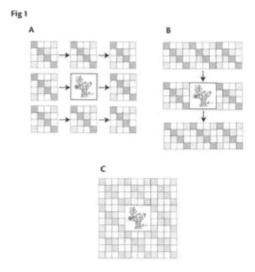

Adding the border

3. From antique dark blue floral cut two 2½in × 12½in (6.3cm × 31.7cm) side borders and two 2½in × 16½in (6.3cm × 42cm) top and bottom borders. Using ¼in (6mm) seam allowances, sew the side borders to the cushion and press (Fig 2). Sew on the top and bottom borders and press. I hand quilted a curly leaf pattern along the border.

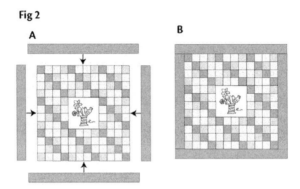

Fig 2

A

B

Assembling the cushion

4. Cut a 16½in (42cm) square from backing fabric and lightweight fusible wadding (batting). Following the manufacturer's directions, iron the wadding on to the wrong sides of both the cushion and the backing.

5. Place the cushion front and back right sides together and stitch around the edge with a ¼in (6mm) seam. Leave a gap of about 4in (10.2cm) at the bottom (Fig 3). Turn the cover through to the right side through the gap, turning out the corners so they are neat and sharp. Press the work gently. Fill the pillow with toy stuffing or use a cushion pad and then stitch up the opening.

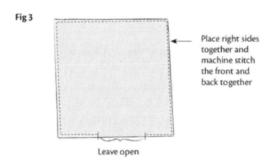

Fig 3

Place right sides together and machine stitch the front and back together

Leave open

CHAPTER 12:

Projects Using Triangles

Chain of Diamonds

Finished block: 2″ × 2″   •   finished quilt: 50″ × 60″

This quilt uses binding triangles: the little corners that are cut off when mitering strips of binding together. The triangles are pieced onto the background blocks in a free-form manner. When the blocks are assembled, the points won't necessarily align, but that is intentional. There is no need to be concerned with precision until it's time to assemble the blocks.

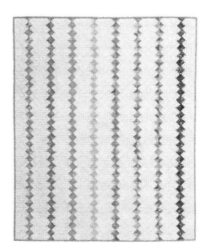

Materials

- White and cream-colored scraps: about 3½ yards total
- 960 binding triangles (see project introduction), or scraps of pink, red, orange, yellow, green, aqua, gray, and black: about ⅓ yard total of each color
- Backing: 3½ yards
- Binding: ⅝ yard
- Cotton batting: 58″ × 68″

Cutting

WOF = width of fabric

White and cream-colored scraps

Cut 750 squares 2½″ × 2½″.

Binding Triangles

Collect 120 binding triangles in each of the following colors: pink, red, orange, yellow, green, aqua, gray, and black or cut 60 squares 2½″ × 2½″ in each of the following colors: pink, red, orange, yellow, green, aqua, gray, and black. Cut squares on the diagonal once, yielding 120 triangles.

Tip

Sizes May Vary

Binding widths generally vary from 2″–2½″ wide. For this quilt, I recommend using triangles cut from 2¼″- and 2½″-wide binding strips for the majority of the pieces.

Triangles from binding strips that are cut 2″ wides may be used for this quilt, but I would recommend mixing them with the larger-size triangles.

Binding

Cut 7 strips 2½″ × WOF.

Make It Faster

If you are using a single background fabric for this quilt, cut nine strips 2½″ × 60½″ and reduce the number of background blocks to 480. Use the 2½″ strips vertically between the columns of pieced blocks.

If you would like to make this quilt but don't want to invest quite as much time as the construction directions require, consider using a larger background block. Start with a 4″ × 4″ or 5″ × 5″ square rather than a 2½″ × 2½″ square. For the colored triangles, use squares up to 1″ smaller than the background block. For example, if you are using a 5″ × 5″ background square, use a 4″ × 4″ square, cut once on the diagonal, for the triangle corners.

Fabric Selection

Various white and cream fabrics were used for the background of this quilt. If you would prefer a cleaner look, use a single fabric for the background. Use a variety of medium and dark values within each strip of color so that the diamonds sparkle. The contrast between the colored strips and the background is important so that the design has maximum impact.

Construction

All seam allowances are ¼″ unless otherwise noted.

1. Place a colored triangle on top of a white background square, right sides together. Before sewing, fold the triangle over the corner to make sure that it will cover the entire corner of the background square. Remember to account for the seam allowance. Sew ¼″ from the diagonal edge of the triangle.

2. Fold the triangle back to cover the corner of the background fabric and press. All of the corner background fabric should be covered by the colored triangle. If some of the background fabric is still visible in the corner, the triangle will need to be repositioned and sewn again.

Correct triangle placement

Incorrect triangle placement

3. Trim, leaving a ¼″ seam allowance. Fold the colored triangle back to cover the trimmed corner and press well.

4. Place another colored triangle on the unit from Step 3, right sides together. Double-check the placement to ensure the triangle will cover the entire corner of the background fabric. Sew ¼″ from the diagonal edge of the triangle.

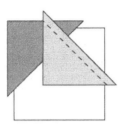

5. Check that the triangle will cover the entire corner and then trim the background fabric from behind the second colored triangle, leaving a ¼″ seam allowance.

Fold the colored triangle back in place and press well. Trim the block to 2½″ × 2½″.

6. Repeat Steps 1–5 to make a total of 60 blocks in each of the colors.

7. Arrange the blocks in a pleasing manner, using the quilt assembly diagram as a guide.

8. Sew the blocks into rows. Follow the arrows for pressing directions. Sew the rows together to complete the quilt top. Press the quilt top well.

Finishing

1. Sew around the perimeter of the quilt top ⅛″ from the edge. This will prevent the seams from splitting during handling before it is quilted.

2. Piece the back to measure at least 58″ × 68″.

3. Baste, quilt, and bind, using your preferred methods. Label if you wish.

4. Wash and dry.

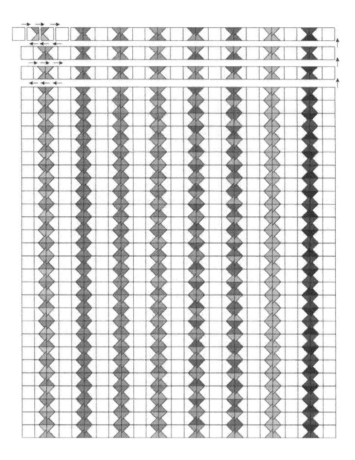

Remainders

Finished block: 2½″ × 2½″   •   finished quilt: 60″ × 75″

A few years ago, I was sewing at a quilt retreat. A friend who was sewing next to me asked if I wanted the trimmings from her snowball blocks. Of course, I wouldn't say no! Most of the triangles measured about 2″ on the shortest side. They are tiny but oh so lovely, and they were the starting point for this quilt.

Materials

- 720 triangle scraps in medium/dark values: about 1¼ yards total
- 720 triangle scraps in light values: about 1¼ yards total

- Background: cream-colored scraps, about 6½–7 yards total
- Backing: 4¾ yards
- Binding: ⅝ yard
- Cotton batting: 68″ × 83″

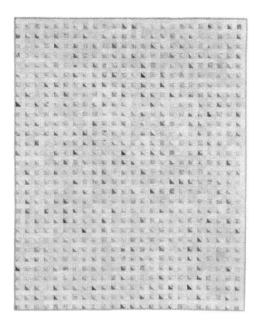

Cutting

WOF = width of fabric

TRIANGLE SCRAPS

Each triangle should measure about 2″ on the shorter sides of the triangle.

Cut (or collect) 720 triangles in medium/dark values.

Cut (or collect) 720 triangles in light values.

The triangles may be a bit larger or a bit smaller than 2″; the slight variation in size adds interest to the quilt. If you don't have triangle trimmings, start by cutting 2″ × 2″ squares and then cut them on the diagonal once to make the triangles.

Cream-Colored Background Scraps

Cut strips 2¼″ wide from different cream-colored fabrics. Lengths may vary.

Binding

Cut eight strips 2½″ × WOF.

Make It Faster

If you prefer a quicker method, use larger pieces. For the triangles, try starting with a 2½″ × 2½″ square rather than a 2″× 2″ square. Increase the cut size of the border strips to 3″ wide. Trim the blocks to 4½″ × 4½″ square. Or play around with different triangle and border sizes to see what proportions you like. Make several test blocks before cutting out all the pieces of the quilt; then follow the instructions for assembling the quilt.

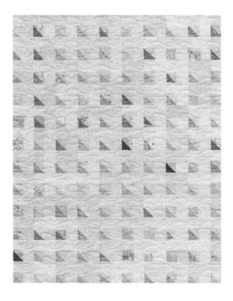

Fabric Selection

The color palette is creamy and muted—a departure from my usual, but I loved the little bits so much that I couldn't pass them up. The colors of the triangles remind me of sea glass. The creams and tans of the background remind me of the sand, which carries out the unintentional beach theme of this quilt.

Construction

All seam allowances are ¼″ unless otherwise noted.

1. Select 1 medium/dark triangle and one light triangle. Place them right sides together and sew along the diagonal edge. Press the seam open or to the side, whichever you prefer. Trim off the tails with sharp scissors or a rotary cutter. Repeat to make 720 half-square triangle (HST) units. The HST units will vary in size but should measure approximately 1⅝″ × 1⅝″ square.

2. Select a cream-colored strip that measures 2¼″ wide and place a half-square triangle unit, right side down, onto the strip in the exact orientation shown below. Sew it in place. Leaving a small gap, place another HST unit down on the strip and sew it in place. Repeat for as many units as will fit on the length of the strip.

Note: Pay attention to the orientation of the triangles when piecing. Always place the medium/dark triangles in the exact orientation shown in the diagrams. This will ensure that the block border strips are sewn to the correct side of the half-square triangle units.

3. Cut the bordered units apart. Press. Trim the excess border so that the strip is the same height as the half-square triangle unit. Repeat for all 720 blocks.

 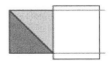 

4. Select a cream-colored 2¼″-wide strip and place a unit from Step 3 on the strip, right side down. Once again, pay close attention to the orientation of the medium/dark triangles. Sew the unit in place. Leave a small gap, then place another unit onto the strip. Repeat for as many units as will fit on the length of the strip. Repeat for all 720 units.

5. Cut the units apart. Press the seams to the side. Trim each to 3″ × 3″ (unfinished), trimming chiefly off the cream-colored sides. Trim as little as possible from the triangle sides. Each half-square triangle block should be bordered on the right and the top. Make 720 blocks.

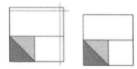

6. Arrange the blocks in a pleasing manner in a 24 by 30 block layout, using the quilt assembly diagram as a guide.

7. Sew the blocks into rows. Follow the arrows for pressing directions. Sew the rows together to complete the quilt top. Press the quilt top well.

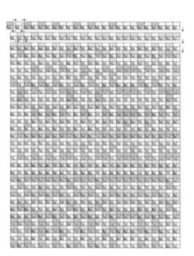

Finishing

1. Sew around the perimeter of the quilt top ⅛″ from the edge. This will prevent the seams from splitting during handling before it is quilted.

2. Piece the back to measure at least 68″ × 83″.

3. Baste, quilt, and bind, using your preferred methods. Label if you wish.

4. Wash and dry.

CHAPTER 13:

Project: William Tell

Finished Quilt: 72½″ × 72½″ • Finished Block: 24″ × 24″

Finished Arrows: Large: 8″ × 24″, Small: 6″ × 24″, Border: 6″ × Varied Lengths

Arrows are appealing. What makes them so appealing is that they are symbolic in several ways.

Cupid comes along and shoots his arrow into someone's heart and he or she falls in love. Many think of arrows as a symbol of our nation's Native American heritage. Others may think of William Tell, the legendary marksman with a crossbow.

This quilt employs a lot of negative space, so the sky's the limit for your creativity. You can use large-scale prints and prints you didn't think you'd use again. There's a monochromatic theme within each arrow. That eliminates a ton of anxiety when choosing fabrics. If one arrow is blue, just pick out a bunch of different blues. They're sure to go together!

Note

- This quilt is made up of 4 large 24″ × 24″ blocks: 2 blocks have 2 large arrows and 2 blocks have 2 small and 1 large arrow.
- The border is made up of small arrows.
- Arrow shafts are appliquéd using your preferred method after the arrow units are pieced.
- Block and border materials and cutting are listed separately.

Materials

For large arrows:

- 3 assorted red scraps, each large enough to yield 4 squares $4\frac{1}{2}″ \times 4\frac{1}{2}″$
- 3 assorted pink scraps, each large enough to yield 4 squares $4\frac{1}{2}″ \times 4\frac{1}{2}″$
- 3 assorted orange scraps, each large enough to yield 4 squares $4\frac{1}{2}″ \times 4\frac{1}{2}″$
- 3 assorted yellow scraps, each large enough to yield 4 squares $4\frac{1}{2}″ \times 4\frac{1}{2}″$
- 3 assorted green scraps, each large enough to yield 4 squares $4\frac{1}{2}″ \times 4\frac{1}{2}″$
- 3 assorted blue scraps, each large enough to yield 4 squares $4\frac{1}{2}″ \times 4\frac{1}{2}″$

For small arrows:

- 3 assorted red scraps, each large enough to yield 4 squares $3\frac{1}{2}″ \times 3\frac{1}{2}″$
- 6 assorted green scraps, each large enough to yield 4 squares $3\frac{1}{2}″ \times 3\frac{1}{2}″$
- 3 assorted blue scraps, each large enough to yield 4 squares $3\frac{1}{2}″ \times 3\frac{1}{2}″$

For arrowheads:

- Assorted gray scraps, enough to yield 12 squares $4\frac{1}{2}″ \times 4\frac{1}{2}″$ and 8 squares $3\frac{1}{2}″ \times 3\frac{1}{2}″$

For arrow shafts:

- Assorted brown scraps, not more than 12 strips $1″ \times 13″$ (amount will vary based on preferred appliqué method)

Other materials

- 3⅛ yards of white for block backgrounds, sashing, and inner border
- 81″ × 81″ backing
- 81″ × 81″ batting
- ⅝ yard for binding

Colored Scraps

Large Arrows

• From each colorway grouping of 3 scraps, cut the following:

4 squares 4½″ × 4½″ per scrap (12 total per colorway; 72 total)

Small Arrows

• From each colorway grouping of 3 scraps, cut the following:

4 squares 3½″ × 3½″ per scrap (12 total per colorway; 48 total)

White

• Cut 19 strips 4½″ × width of fabric.

Sub cut the following:

8 rectangles 4½″ × 24″ for the sashing

48 squares 4½″ × 4½″ for the large arrows

Set the remaining 8 strips aside for the row sashing and inner border.

Small Arrows

• Cut 5 strips 3½″ × width of fabric.

Sub cut 48 squares 3½″ × 3½″.

Gray scraps

Large Arrows

• Cut 6 pairs of matching squares 4½″ × 4½″ (12 total).

Small Arrows

• Cut 4 pairs of matching squares 3½″ × 3½″ (8 total).

Making the Arrow Blocks

All seam allowances are ¼″. Press toward the darker fabric when making the half-square triangle (HST) units. Follow the arrows for pressing direction.

Use method 2 to make the HST units.

Large Arrow Units

The large arrow units are made of an arrowhead, a shaft, and three feathers. The shaft is appliquéd after the blocks are constructed.

To make one large arrow unit, you will need:

8 white squares 4½″ × 4½″

2 matching gray squares 4½″ × 4½″

3 sets of 4 matching squares 4½″ × 4½″ in the same colorway (A, B, C)

Label the matching squares if needed, or make a key for yourself.

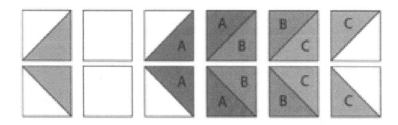

1. For the arrowhead, sew 2 matching white/gray HST units.

2. For the feathers, sew the following HST units:

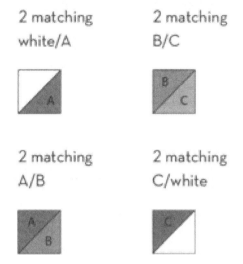

3. Sew all the matching HST units together into pairs, rotating 1 HST unit in each pair as shown. Press.

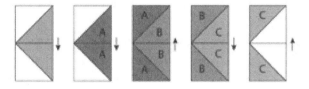

4. Sew 2 white 4½″ × 4½″ squares together. Press.

5. Lay out the paired arrowhead, white, and feather units as shown. Sew together to make a large arrow unit. Press all seams toward the arrowhead.

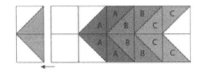

6. Repeat Steps 1–5 to make a total of 6 large arrow units.

Small Arrow Units

The small arrow units are made of an arrowhead, a longer shaft, and three feathers. The shaft is appliquéd after the blocks are constructed.

To make one small arrow unit, you will need:

12 white squares 3½″ × 3½″

2 matching gray squares 3½″ × 3½″

3 sets of 4 matching squares 3½″ × 3½″ in the same colorway (A, B, C)

1. Repeat Large Arrow Units, Steps 1–3, using the 3½″ × 3½″ squares.

2. Sew two white 3½″ × 3½″ squares together. Repeat this step to make a total of 3 white pairs. Press the seams in one direction.

3. Lay out the paired arrowhead, white, and feather units as shown. Rotate the white pairs as needed so the seams nest. Sew together to make a small arrow unit. Press all seams away from the arrowhead.

4. Repeat Steps 1–3 to make a total of 4 small arrow units.

Three-Arrow Blocks

1. Arrange two small arrow units and one large arrow unit with a 4½″ × 24½″ block sashing strip, as shown in the block assembly diagrams.

2. Sew the units together. Press.

3. Repeat Steps 1 and 2 to make a second three-arrow block, as shown.

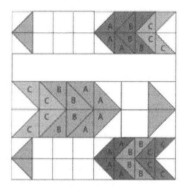

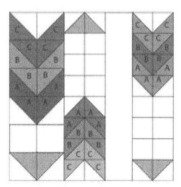

THREE-ARROW BLOCK ASSEMBLY

Two-Arrow Blocks

1. Arrange two large arrow units with two block sashing strips 4½″ × 24½″, as shown in the block assembly diagram.

2. Sew the units together. Press.

3. Repeat Steps 1 and 2 to make a second two-arrow block, as shown.

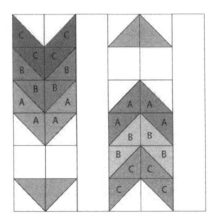

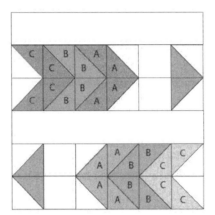

TWO-ARROW BLOCK ASSEMBLY

Making the Borders

All seam allowances are ¼˝. Press toward the darker fabric when making HST units. Follow the arrows for pressing direction.

The outer border is sewn entirely from 3½˝ × 3½˝ squares, but the lengths of the shaft units vary. Shafts will be appliquéd after the borders are constructed.

Use method 2 to make the HST units.

Materials

For border arrows:

- 3 assorted pink scraps, each large enough to yield 4 squares $3\frac{1}{2}'' \times 3\frac{1}{2}''$
- 3 assorted red scraps #1, each large enough to yield 4 squares $3\frac{1}{2}'' \times 3\frac{1}{2}''$
- 3 assorted red scraps #2, each large enough to yield 4 squares $3\frac{1}{2}'' \times 3\frac{1}{2}''$
- 4 assorted yellow scraps, each large enough to yield 4 squares $3\frac{1}{2}'' \times 3\frac{1}{2}''$
- 3 assorted green scraps, each large enough to yield 4 squares $3\frac{1}{2}'' \times 3\frac{1}{2}''$
- 3 assorted blue scraps #1, each large enough to yield 4 squares $3\frac{1}{2}'' \times 3\frac{1}{2}''$
- 3 assorted blue scraps #2, each large enough to yield 4 squares $3\frac{1}{2}'' \times 3\frac{1}{2}''$
- 3 assorted purple scraps #1, each large enough to yield 4 squares $3\frac{1}{2}'' \times 3\frac{1}{2}''$
- 4 assorted purple scraps #2, each large enough to yield 4 squares $3\frac{1}{2}'' \times 3\frac{1}{2}''$
- 4 assorted brown scraps, each large enough to yield 4 squares $3\frac{1}{2}'' \times 3\frac{1}{2}''$

Other materials

- Assorted gray scraps, enough to yield 20 squares $3\frac{1}{2}'' \times 3\frac{1}{2}''$ for arrowheads
- $1\frac{3}{8}$ yards white for background

Colored scraps

From each colorway grouping of 3 or 4 scraps, cut the following:

- 4 squares $3\frac{1}{2}'' \times 3\frac{1}{2}''$ per scrap (12 or 16 per colorway; 132 total).

Gray scraps

- Cut 10 pairs of matching squares $3\frac{1}{2}'' \times 3\frac{1}{2}''$ (20 total).

White

- Cut 12 strips $3\frac{1}{2}'' \times$ width of fabric. Subcut 130 squares $3\frac{1}{2}'' \times 3\frac{1}{2}''$.

Top Border

1. Follow Small Arrow Units to make a red border arrow unit and a green border arrow unit, but only use two pairs of white 3½″ × 3½″ squares, as shown.

2. Sew 3 four-patches of white 3½″ × 3½″ squares. Press seams in alternate directions so they nest.

3. Sew the two border arrows and three four-patches together as shown to make the top border. Rotate the four-patches as needed so the seams will nest.

TOP BORDER

Bottom Border

1. Follow Small Arrow Units to make a pink border arrow, but only use two pairs of white 3½″ × 3½″ squares, as shown.

2. Follow Small Arrow Units to make a brown border arrow, but make an additional colored HST unit and 4 pairs of white 3½″ × 3½″ squares, as shown.

3. Sew 2 white 3½″ × 3½″ squares together to make a two-patch. Press.

4. Sew 1 four-patch of white 3½″ × 3½″ squares. Press seams in alternate directions so they nest.

5. Sew the 2 border arrows and white two- and four-patches together as shown to make the bottom border. Rotate the white units as needed so the seams will nest.

BOTTOM BORDER

Left Border

1. Follow Small Arrow Units to make a red border arrow.

2. Follow Small Arrow Units to make a blue border arrow, but only use 1 pair of white $3\frac{1}{2}'' \times 3\frac{1}{2}''$ squares, as shown.

3. Follow Small Arrow Units to make a purple border arrow, but make an additional colored HST unit and only use two pairs of white $3\frac{1}{2}'' \times 3\frac{1}{2}''$ squares, as shown.

4. Sew two white $3\frac{1}{2}'' \times 3\frac{1}{2}''$ squares together to make a two-patch. Press.

5. Sew a four-patch of white $3\frac{1}{2}'' \times 3\frac{1}{2}''$ squares. Press seams in alternate directions so they nest.

6. Sew the two border arrows and white two- and four-patches together as shown to make the left side border. Rotate the white units as needed so the seams will nest.

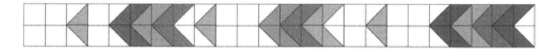

LEFT SIDE BORDER

Right Border

1. Follow Small Arrow Units to make a blue border arrow and a purple border arrow, but only use 1 pair of white $3\frac{1}{2}'' \times 3\frac{1}{2}''$ squares, as shown.

2. Follow Small Arrow Units to make a yellow border arrow, but make an additional colored HST unit and only use 2 pairs of white $3\frac{1}{2}'' \times 3\frac{1}{2}''$ squares, as shown.

3. Sew 2 white $3\frac{1}{2}'' \times 3\frac{1}{2}''$ squares together to make a two-patch. Repeat to make a second two-patch. Press.

4. Sew a four-patch of white $3\frac{1}{2}'' \times 3\frac{1}{2}''$ squares. Press seams in alternate directions so they nest.

5. Sew the 2 border arrows and white two- and four-patches together as shown to make the right side border. Rotate the white units as needed so the seams will nest.

RIGHT SIDE BORDER

Putting It All Together

1. Refer to the quilt assembly diagram to sew the arrow blocks together in 2 rows of 2 with a $4\frac{1}{2}"$ × $24\frac{1}{2}"$ sashing strip between them.

2. Sew the 8 remaining $4\frac{1}{2}"$ × width of fabric strips together ends to end for the horizontal sashing and inner border. Press.

3. Cut a strip $4\frac{1}{2}"$ × $52\frac{1}{2}"$ for the horizontal sashing. Sew the 2 rows together with the sashing.

4. Refer to How to Accurately Apply Borders to measure, cut, and attach the inner border.

The side borders should measure $52\frac{1}{2}"$ long and the top and bottom should be $60\frac{1}{2}"$.

The inner border is sewn to the sides first and then the top and bottom. Press toward the center.

5. Sew the top and bottom arrow borders to the quilt. Press. Sew the left and right-side arrow borders to the quilt. Press toward the center.

Adding the Arrow Shafts

1. Cut brown strips (with or without seam allowances, depending on your chosen appliqué method), so the finished width after appliquéing is approximately $\frac{1}{2}"$.

2. Appliqué the brown strips to the quilt top between the arrowheads and the feather unit of the arrows, using your preferred method.

Finishing

Layer, baste, quilt, and bind as desired.

QUILT ASSEMBLY

CHAPTER 14:

Negative Space

Tips for Quilting Negative Space

- Decide how much you want the quilting to show.
- Try using the designs in different ways.
- Play around.

Peapods

Sometimes the easiest way to come up with a quilting design is to combine some of your favorite designs. Peapods does that by combining pebbles and serpentine lines. This design is fantastic because the quilting can be small and dense or large and airy. It works well in smaller background areas of quilts and larger negative space.

Start/stop

1. Start by quilting a gentle serpentine line that goes out and echoes back to a point.

2. Echo the sides of the shape, touching the end point and returning to the starting point.

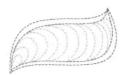

3. Fill inside the peapod shape with a filler. For this example, I filled the pod with arcs. End at the opposite point.

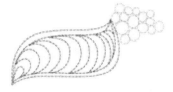

4. Fill around the peapod with pebbles.

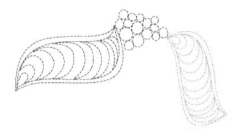

5. Once you have covered enough space, quilt another peapod.

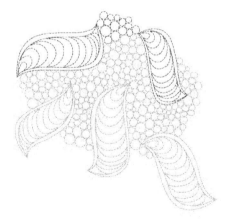

6. Continue quilting pods and your filler quilting design until the area is filled.

Tip

Since the peapods are larger than the pebbles, quilt peapods first and then fill around them with the pebbles.

Offset Squares

Want a more geometric look for your quilts? This design is for you! It's a spin on the square chain quilting design and the only difference is the layout of the squares. It's best for larger areas of negative space and is easy to quilt. You can make the offset squares as small or as large as you want.

Before starting, let's talk about the square we will be using. Starting from one side, quilt the outside of a box and keep echoing inside until you get to the center. From the center, go across the previously quilted lines so that you'll be in position to quilt the next square.

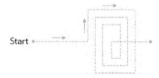

Now let's learn how to offset the squares and give them a neat, tailored-to-fit look.

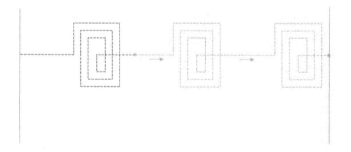

1. Working your way across the quilting area, quilt the squares with spaces in between. Try to keep these spaces roughly the same size as the outermost square.

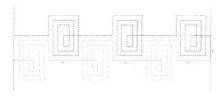

2. Travel down the edge of the quilting area until you are about ½″ below the bottom of the last square. Work back across the quilting area, offsetting this row of squares to fit into the spaces you left as you quilted the preceding row.

3. Continue until the whole area is filled.

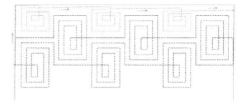

4. When quilting the top and bottom of the quilting area, quilt smaller blocks to fill in the spaces.

Swirl Chain

Swirls are the ultimate quilting design. You can use them in so many different ways and so many areas of the quilt. The swirl chain takes the basic swirl and pumps it up a notch.

This design looks anything but basic and is perfect for filling large areas of negative space.

1. Starting from the edge of the quilting area, quilt an elongated swirl and echo back to the edge.

2. Travel up the edge about ¼″, echo outside the swirl from Step 1, and echo back to return to the edge again.

3. Travel up the edge about ¼″ and quilt an elongated swirl that goes out and above the one you quilted in Steps 1 and 2. Return to the edge.

4. Travel up the edge about ¼″ and then echo around the swirl from Step 3 so that you are pausing at the point where the 2 swirls meet.

5. Quilt a teardrop shape and echo it. This is an optional step; you could omit the teardrop if you would like.

6. Quilt the next swirl so it goes under the preceding swirl. Echo the preceding swirl partly, and then create another swirl, ending at the point where the 2 swirls meet.

7. Add a teardrop and quilt the next swirl as you did in Steps 5 and 6.

8. Continue quilting the swirls until you reach the other side of the quilting area.

Tip

When quilting this design, if you find yourself on the wrong side of the swirl, just echo around it until you get to the desired side. By the time you fill in around the design, you won't even notice the extra lines!

Links

Although it might not be obvious at first, this design is actually a variation of the classic clamshell quilting design.

It is made up of two basic shapes and is fast and easy to quilt. It works in blocks, borders, or even as an allover quilting design.

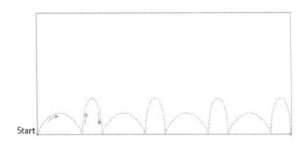

1. Starting at the bottom of the quilting area, quilt a row of arcs. After that, alternate between short, wide arcs and tall, skinny arcs. As a general guide, the shorter ones should be about twice as wide and half as tall. End when you get to the edge of the quilting area.

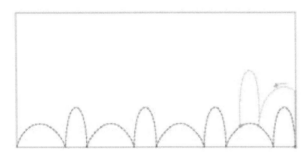

2. Travel up the edge of the quilting area and echo over the top of the skinny arc. Then quilt a skinny arc centered over the wider arc.

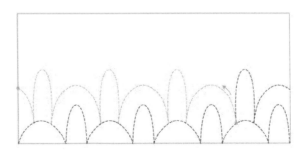

3. Work your way across the quilting area, echoing over the skinny arcs and quilting skinny arcs above the wider arcs.

Make sure that the skinny arcs that you quilt on this row are taller than the echoed lines.

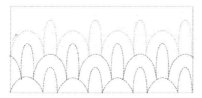

4. Continue quilting the rows by repeating the arcs and echoed lines.

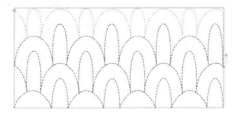

5. When you reach the top of the quilting area, make the skinny arcs short enough to fill in the top completely.

Tip

Change up the size to quilt quicker! Making the design larger means that you can quilt more and faster.

Merged Lines

Who knew that echoing straight lines would look so appealing? This design adds a simple but groovy look to your quilt.

This one works spectacularly in all sizes of negative space or as an allover design. You may be tempted to get out the ruler.

1. Start a few inches from the top of the quilting area and quilt a horizontal line toward the opposite side. At a random point, quilt a diagonal line at about 45° and then continue quilting horizontally until you reach the other side.

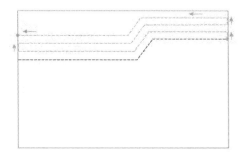

2. Before quilting the rest of the area, fill in above the line, by echoing the first line. For this design, I normally echo about ½˝ apart.

3. You can also echo only a portion of the line. For instance, instead of echoing the diagonal portion of the line, echo just the horizontal part.

Travel along the previously quilted diagonal line and return to the edge.

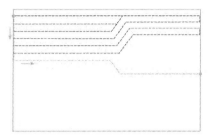

4. Once the top of the area is filled, it's time to quilt the line that will set off the next portion. Travel along the edge so that you are about ½″ below the first line, and quilt another horizontal line, randomly going down at an angle and then continuing horizontally until you reach the edge.

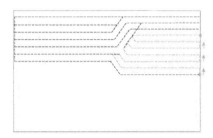

5. Fill in the area between the two lines by echoing. Be sure to travel along the edge of the quilting area or previously quilted lines, as shown.

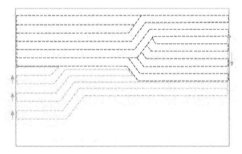

6. After you have filled in the area, travel along the edge of the quilting area and repeat the technique in Steps 1–5.

7. Continue until the quilting area is completely filled.

Wavy Wavy

Wavy shows that a simple design can add movement and texture to your quilt. It's just an added bonus that it's so easy to quilt. This design is perfect for medium to large areas of negative space or as an allover quilting design.

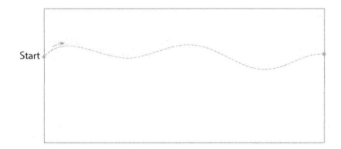

1. Starting a few inches below the top of the quilting area, quilt a gently waving line from one side to the other.

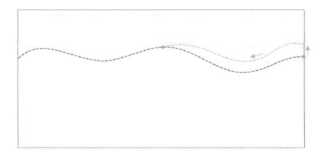

2. Travel up the edge of the quilting area about ½˝. Quilt a wavy line that echoes the first wavy line. At a random point while echoing, run into the line below.

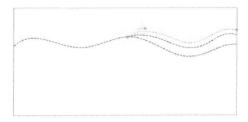

3. Quilt a line echoing back the opposite direction, returning to the edge.

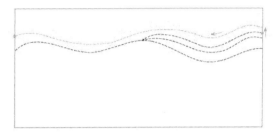

4. Travel up the edge of the quilting area and then echo across to the other edge of the quilting area. Traveling along the edge ensures that your lines will stay somewhat horizontal.

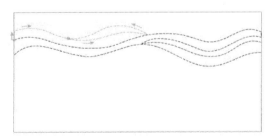

5. Work your way back across the quilt, running into the line below.

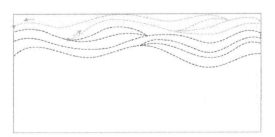

6. Repeat the technique in Steps 1–5, filling in the area.

7. Travel down along the edge until you are about ½″ below the first line (from Step 1). Repeat the technique in Steps 1–6 to fill in the quilting area.

Tip

You can add more movement with this design by running into lines more often.

Jumbled Lines

While quilting this design, you are basically dividing up the quilting areas into smaller squares and filling them in.

1. Starting from the side of the quilting area, quilt two sides of a rectangle.

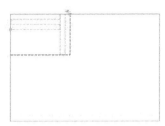

2. Begin filling in the rectangle, alternating between horizontal and vertical lines. Travel along the previously quilted lines.

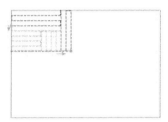

3. Continue until the unit is filled. End so that you are at a corner of the rectangle.

Tip

If you get stuck, no worries! Just travel along a line of quilting to get where you need to be.

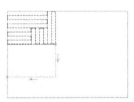

4. Quilt the sides of another rectangle that touches the first one that you quilted.

5. Fill in the rectangle by alternating between horizontal and vertical lines, as you did in Step 2.

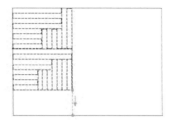

6. When you get to the bottom of the quilting area, you may need to quilt only one line to create the next unit.

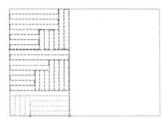

7. Travel along the edge of the quilting area; quilt another rectangle and fill in with lines.

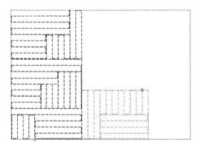

8. Continue until the quilting area is completely filled.

Tips for quilting straight lines

- If using a longarm quilting machine, you may want to use a ruler. But I find that if I am quilting shorter lines, I can usually freehand it.

- Using a matching color of a thread will help cover any bumps and wobbles.

Back-And-Forth Lines

This scalable design can be quilted as small or as large as you like. Try it in small areas of negative space or as a quick way to fill up larger areas of negative space. Use the back-and-forth lines around appliquéd blocks or quilting motifs to make them pop! As you can see, there are so many different ways to use it!

1. Starting in the corner of the quilting area, quilt a column of back-and-forth lines that almost touch the edge but are varying widths. Work your way to the bottom of the quilting area.

2. At the bottom of the quilting area, begin quilting another column of back-and-forth lines, working your way back up the quilt. Make each of the lines varying widths, but make the lines on one side close to the lines of the previous column.

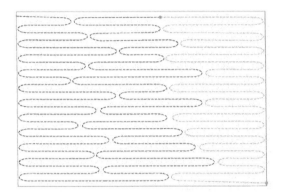

3. Depending on the size of your quilting area, continue quilting columns of back-and-forth lines. When you get to the edge of the quilting area, quilt the lines so they fit in the remaining space.

CHAPTER 15:

Ovals

A close cousin of circles, ovals can be used in many of the same ways to create different effects.

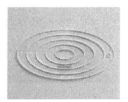

Unlike circles, which have a uniform curve all the way around, ovals feature curves that change as you move around the shape. You can use different parts of the curve to get a variety of effects.

To quilt consistent motifs in multiple blocks can be helpful to mark the ruler with tape or a permanent marker to ensure you are stitching along the same part of the curve each time.

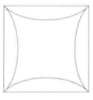

Design featuring the flatter side of an oval

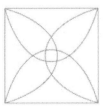

Design featuring the more curved side of an oval

Overlapping Cathedral Windows

This border design is as quick and easy as they come! It quickly covers a large space with minimal marking.

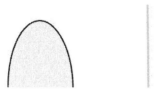

1. Choose an oval ruler that, when oriented vertically with its centerline aligned with the border seam, will stitch an arc slightly shorter than the border's width. Mark a vertical line at the center of the border.

2. Measure the shorter dimension of the oval and add ½˝ to that measurement. Working from the center out, make marks at even intervals across the bottom of the border this distance apart.

3. Aligning the etched lines on the oval with the base of the border, quilt from side to side to connect the marks (you may have to quilt a compensating motif at the sides of the border).

4. Make a second set of marks the same distance apart in between the first.

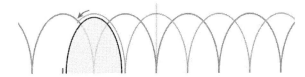

5. Add another layer of complexity to the design by working back across the border.

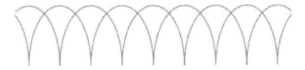

6. Continue until you reach the other side.

Free-Motion Fill: Overlapping Cathedral Windows

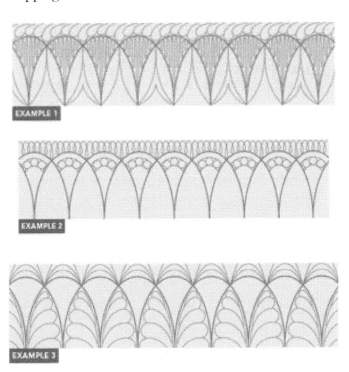

Cathedral Windows

This is a border design to try. Baste in the ditch along the edge of the border before quilting the motifs to keep the edge from being distorted.

To keep the motif appearing consistent, try to quilt along the same part of the oval curve each time.

If you prefer, you can also quilt one window in the center of the border and work outward.

1. Choose an oval ruler that, when oriented vertically with its centerline aligned with the border seam, will stitch an arc roughly the height of the border.

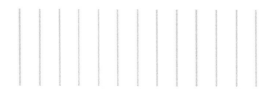

2. Mark a vertical line at the center of the border. Divide the narrower dimension of the oval in half. Working from the center out, mark vertical lines at even intervals across the bottom of the border at a slightly narrower distance apart (the smaller the distance, the narrower and spikier the windows will be).

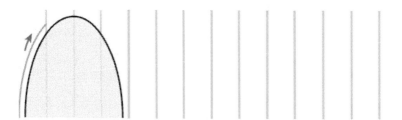

3. Aligning the etched lines on the oval with the base of the border, quilt from the base of a vertical line up to the next vertical line. (You may have to quilt a compensating motif at the sides of the border.)

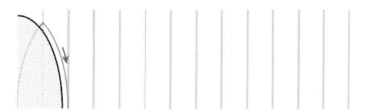

4. Quilt down to the base of the next vertical line, realigning the ruler to use its other side.

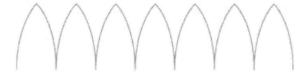

5. Continue until you complete the border.

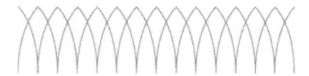

To add another layer of complexity to the design, make a second set of marks in between the first, and connect them.

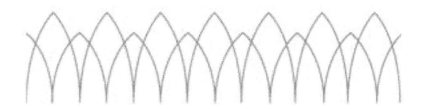

If you'd like, you can even make this second pass a different height by adjusting the tilt or size of the ruler.

Free-Motion Fill: Cathedral Windows

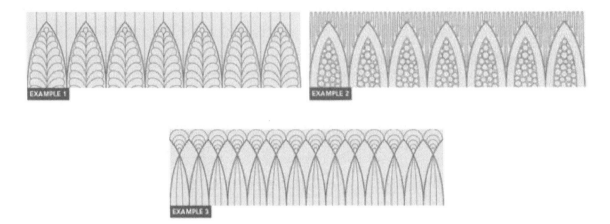

Oval Petals and Diamonds

This design is quick and looks marvelous at both a small scale (in sashing) and a large scale (in a border embellished with free-motion). If you prefer, you can center a motif in the middle of the border and work outward from its edges. Oval Petals and Diamonds can also be worked as an allover fill.

1. Choose an oval ruler that, when oriented horizontally with its centerline aligned with the border seam, will stitch an arc roughly three-quarters the height of the border. Mark a vertical line at the center of the border.

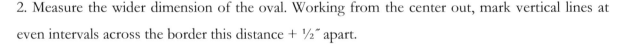

2. Measure the wider dimension of the oval. Working from the center out, mark vertical lines at even intervals across the border this distance + ½″ apart.

3. Aligning the etched lines on the oval with the base of the border, quilt from the base of a vertical line to the base of the next (you may have to quilt a compensating motif at the sides of the border).

4. Continue across the border.

5. Quilt along the side of the border and quilt the upper half of the design, aligning the etched lines on the oval with the top of the border (if you are quilting the edge of a quilt with this design, make sure to allow for binding).

6. Continue until you complete the border.

You can get a variety of results by using different sizes of ovals on different border widths.

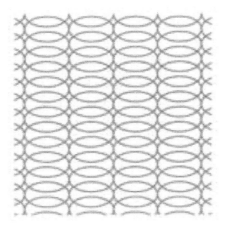

This pattern can be done in rows as an allover fill.

Free-Motion Fill: Oval Petals and Diamonds

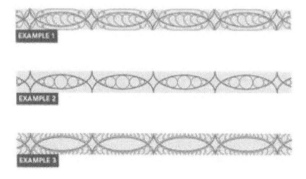

Oval Clamshells

This is a wonderful allover design for both modern and traditional quilt tops. It can be done at both a small and large scale. Clamshells are great traditional and modern fills!

1. Choose an oval ruler to establish the size of the clamshells. Make marks at even intervals across the bottom of the quilt the same distance apart as the oval's wider dimension + ½″.

2. Quilt to connect the marks, aligning the center of the oval on the edge of the quilting area.

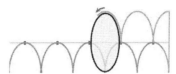

3. Use the top of the first row of clamshells to line up the bottom of the next row of clamshells. If desired, mark a horizontal line at the top of the arc and the center of each. (Or be lazy like me and just wing it!) Quilt up the side of the quilting area and connect the marks, aligning the quarter marks on the ruler with the former stitching.

4. Continue until you finish the design.

Change the orientation of the oval ruler for a different look!

Try tilting and mirroring the ovals for another variation.

Oval Connecting Corners

Think about using ovals as you would use circles to embellish blocks. Designs evocative of a flower will appear. Try variations—you'll be pleasantly surprised at the results!

1. Mark the center of the block.

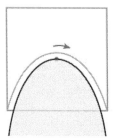

2. Quilt from one corner to the next, using the more curved side of an oval and making sure that the edge of the ruler is ¼″ from the block corners. For a uniform curve, the oval ruler must be

oriented squarely to the block edge (your block center might be in a different location relative to the ruler than what is shown). If you notice the ruler has slipped when you're halfway across the curve, correct it before continuing.

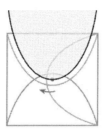

3. Paying attention to the consistency with which the oval is aligned with the block's center point to ensure a uniform design, continue around the block.

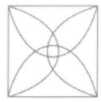

4. until you get back to the starting point.

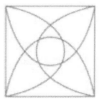

Try varying the size of the oval.

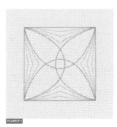

Free-Motion Fill: Oval Connecting Corners

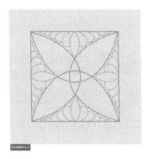

Oval Connecting Sides

Yet another variation using ovals … so fun to embellish with free-motion!

1. Mark the center of each side of the block.

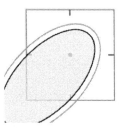

2. Audition oval rulers to find a ruler whose narrower measurement + ½˝ is equal to or slightly greater than the distance between the block's side center points.

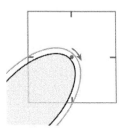

3. Stitch along the ruler to connect the center point of one side with the center point of the next.

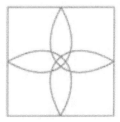

4. Continue around the block until you get back to the starting point (to ensure a uniform design, pay attention to the consistency with which the oval is aligned with the block's center point).

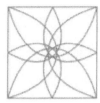

Combine this design with Oval Connecting Corners for a unique look.

Free-Motion Fill: Oval Connecting Sides

Ovals in A Column

Ovals look great running down a quilt. They add organic curves and a more rigid structure at the same time. You can quilt them all over, or quilt them in just a portion of the quilt and embellish the design with free-motion. Make sure your quilt following the figure-eight curve as shown. If you quilt rows of scallops instead, it can be difficult to align the marks on the next pass!

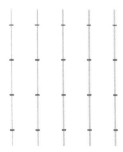

1. Mark a vertical line down the center of the quilting area. Mark additional evenly spaced lines on either side, far enough apart that the ovals will not touch. Measure the oval's wider dimension and make marks at even intervals down the lines this distance + ½˝ apart.

2. Aligning the oval ruler markings to the vertical line, quilt around one side of the ruler and then the other (you may need to quilt a compensating motif at the edge of the quilt top).

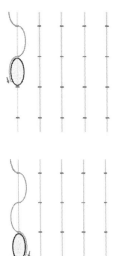

3. Continue down the quilting area, alternating holding the ruler on the left and right to begin forming a figure-eight shape.

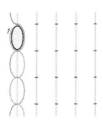

4. Travel back from right to left to complete the figure-eight.

5. Working from the center out, stitch columns of ovals to fill the quilting area.

You can do as I like to and stitch another pass using the same marks but a larger oval ruler.

Try offsetting some of the rows.

Try doing a second offset pass on each one for a lovely allover pattern!

The ovals can be rotated for a different look

or the entire design can be rotated.

Try quilting the columns closer together.

Oval Grid

Take advantage of the directional nature of ovals to quilt an eye-catching grid. There are so many variations possible!

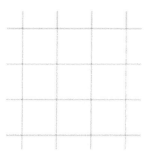

1. Draw a grid of horizontal and vertical lines on the quilt top. Each grid square should be equal to the oval's wider dimension + ½˝.

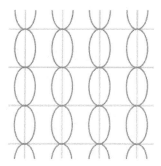

2. Refer to Ovals in a Column to quilt columns of ovals, centered on each vertical line.

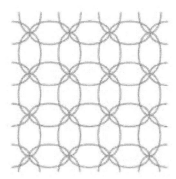

3. Quilt rows of ovals in the same manner.

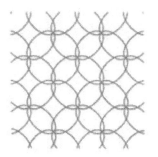

Free-Motion Fill: Oval Grid

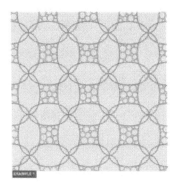

Conclusion

Quilting has a long history, and, it would seem, a great long future. The customs of the early quilters have not been lost, and they have been taken throughout the world. British women took their abilities and customs to the opposite side of the world, to America and Australia. American quilters in the twentieth century are accountable for carrying this craft into the twenty-first century all over the world.

The Hawaiian folks record their history through their quilts and reveal the world their religious and spiritual past and present.

The French have utilized quilting as a medium for their creative drive and have actually created a few of the gorgeous quilts, with elaborate and creative stitching.

Japanese clothing has customarily consisted of quilt work, and the fantastic silks of the kimono can be wonderfully elegant when appliquéd and quilted.

South Africa, as well, has a great love affair with quilting, and the colors and patterns demonstrate the environment, its colors and its wildlife.

There are quilts around the world that have stayed in identical households for generations, and there are quilts shown in museums and exhibits, in town halls, in hotels, in company workplaces and dining establishments.

Every great work starts with a single step. This is true indeed for those people who wanted to learn the art of quilting. This book is a perfect tool for beginners to learn the few essential skills needed in quilting.

Quilting is not a complicated art to learn but needs determination and enough perseverance to achieve the necessary skills in creating a beautiful quilt work. Beginners should not lose heart when the intended format cannot be achieved because with the help of this book, you will be able to learn the correct way to achieve your goals.

Quilting for beginners is indeed a very productive past time because it is a potential source of income for some. With the help of this book, beginners should be able to utilize the basic steps in creating different beautiful creations from the beginner's skillful hand.

Quilting can be straightforward or complicated patchwork; it can be the most splendid stitchery on simple or pricey fabrics. You can quilt a little cushion cover, a bed cover, a purse, a small, medium or big wall hanging. You can utilize painted or dyed fabrics, and you can include motifs, appliqués or integrate ribbons, pearls or diamonds.

There is nearly any design, any size and any use for a quilt.

Quilting can be a bit overwhelming at first sight, especially if you do not have any idea of where and how to start. This book will provide you with so many kinds of information that you can use to start quilting from what materials you need to choose the right fabric and from laying out a pattern to sewing the fabrics together.

I hope that you enjoyed reading through this book and that you have found it useful. Have a great rest of the day.

Printed in Great Britain
by Amazon

61548602R10081